SUFI RAPPER

The Spiritual Journey of Abd al Malik

ABD AL MALIK

Translated by Jon E. Graham

Inner Traditions
Rochester, Vermont

Inner Traditions
One Park Street
Rochester, Vermont 05767
www.InnerTraditions.com

Originally published in French under the title *Qu'Allah bénisse la France!* by Éditions Albin
Michel S.A., Paris
First U.S. edition published in 2009 by Inner Traditions

Library of Congress Cataloging-in-Publication Data
Abd al Malik, 1975–
  [Qu'Allah bénisse la France! English]
  Sufi rapper : the spiritual journey of Abd al Malik / Abd al Malik ; translated by Jon E.
Graham.—1st U.S. ed.
      p. cm.
  "Originally published in French under the title Qu'Allah bénisse la France! by Éditions
Albin Michel S.A., Paris."
  Summary: "French rap star recounts his journey from the ghettos of Paris through radical
Islam to the Sufi message of universal love"—Provided by publisher.
  ISBN 978-1-59477-278-8 (pbk.)
  1. Abd al Malik, 1975– 2. Rap musicians—France—Biography. 3. Muslims—France—
Biography. I. Title.
  ML420.A12A3 2009
  782.421649092—dc22
  [B]
                                                                        2008050151

Printed and bound in the United States by Lake Book Manufacturing

10 9 8 7 6 5 4 3 2 1

Text design by Virginia Scott Bowman and layout by Priscilla Baker
This book was typeset in Garamond Premier Pro with Impact used as a display typeface

Inner Traditions wishes to express its appreciation for assistance given by the government
of France through the National Book Office of the Ministère de la Culture in the
preparation of this translation.

Nous tenons à exprimer nos plus vifs remerciements au government de la France et le
ministère de la Culture, Centre National du Livre, pour leur concours dans le préparation
de la traduction de cet ouvrage.

SUFI RAPPER

To my mother, who made me the man I am today,
And to my father, whom I've rediscovered. . . .

CONTENTS

ACKNOWLEDGMENTS

In homage to my guide Sidi Hamza al Qadiri al Butchichi, who is teaching me, in the intimacy of our hearts, how to be a universal man filled with love for all humanity.

Thank you, Sidi, for bringing me back to life in this life.

I also thank Wallen, Nadir, Rachid, Bachir, and especially Jean and Julien . . . without whose valuable assistance I could never have written this book.

There are certain people who might feel offended by some of the remarks made about them in this book, and I offer my sincere apologies for this. But this is my life story: I have to tell it.

ONE

TWO LIVES FOR THE PRICE OF ONE

Yesterday this Black, it was me typical example of a
  certain kind of thug
There was a moat, a wall, a universe between you and me
Yesterday I wanted to burn it all down, the bourgeois I
  detested
I picked this Fabien clean I got turned on seeing the
  Whitey flip out
Give me all you got on you or else I'll stab you dead
  "loser"
That will be a change for you huh, you are only a dirty
  petit-bourgeois
Yesterday I did not understand his life but after this scene
I kept my hatred because we are poor and you are not

FROM THE SONG "BLACK & WHITE"

I was already three years old when I was born in the fourteenth arrondissement of Paris. Régis was my baptized name. I was barely two years old when my father, a member of the Vili people, was called back

1

to his native land of Congo to assume a high government post there, after having obtained his diploma in political science in France. He was invited to be one of the future advisors to the prime minister. My mother, a member of the Teke people, who had immigrated to France against her will and suffered from homesickness, was delighted about this almost unhoped-for return.

I say that I was already three years old when I was born because on October 11, 1978, my brother Fayette came into the world and I have no memory of anything I may have experienced before this day. Everything after it, however, remains perfectly etched in my mind. Fayette chose to enter the world at the Blanche Gomez Civil Hospital of Brazzaville, Congo.

I can still clearly see myself in that hospital room at whose center my mother, still wearing white and lying down, was talking in hushed tones with my father and my uncle. I was still trying to grasp the object of their enigmatic conversation when my brother Arnaud, who is three years older than me, gave me a huge smile and tugged at my sleeve to show me his discovery. I looked around and finally understood what was happening: curled up in my mother's arms, all crumpled with sleek hair and so tiny I had not seen him, was the center of all the attention. So another person was now here! This was my introduction to the mystery of life.

We lived in a neighborhood of government housing in Brazzaville, the same quarter where most of the state dignitaries had their homes. I spent my time there on incessant escapades and epic games around the guava trees that bordered our building. It was necessary to take as much advantage of the day as possible, especially as numerous electrical breakdowns would often plunge our quarter into darkness once evening fell. The cutoff of the electricity generally occurred around the time of dinner, which we would then finish beneath the stars. The frequency of these inconveniences did not diminish the effect of surprise they caused, which inspired a state of laughing excitement and joy in Arnaud and me, while the adults calmly got things under control.

One of my parents would grope through the apartment to the utility room and come back with candles, matches, or lighter, as well as a small tin candleholder. Our father or our Uncle Paul—who was living with us—then brought us back out to the large balcony where we had been eating several minutes earlier, before the darkness scattered us. The inhabitants of the entire quarter could be seen on their balconies. Like us, they were bathed in moonlight and displayed not the slightest sign of panic or aggravation. The memory of these magic moments still fills me with the muffled and soothing atmosphere that accompanied them.

We often went to Pointe-Noire, the economic capital located in the southern part of the country, where a large part of my father's family lived. I remember how, during the course of one of our many strolls along the beaches there, which were bathed by the Atlantic Ocean, Arnaud found a fish that had washed up and, taking advantage of the momentary inattention of one of our aunts who was accompanying us, stuffed it into his pocket. On the path home he whispered to me that he intended to cook it once the grown-ups had begun their siesta. Of course, once we arrived at our aunt's house, the dead fish stunk so bad that Arnaud was quickly found out. Through his tears, he explained the reason for his action, causing my aunt to burst into laughter. Even now, more than twenty-five years later, she finds it just as amusing.

I can still remember Poto-Poto in the Brazzaville suburbs, where my mother's family lived. There, with my grandparents, uncles, aunts, and especially my cousins, we spent radiant days filled with light and joy. These moments remain forever associated in my mind with love of family and the Congo. I realize today that my formative years as a small child took place in an atmosphere that encouraged respect for adults; it was an atmosphere of emotional stability. Later, I was to learn that many of my French black friends, those who had never known Africa, did not enjoy this same sense of emotional peace and well-being.

I experienced those years like a wonderful journey, the light and laughing memories of which reflect the happiest period of my life. But

I knew that I was on a journey, in a purely transitory but eminently agreeable situation. Arnaud and I carefully arranged our room every morning, convinced we were living through a long vacation that would inevitably be followed by a return "home"—in other words, France. During the course of the summer of 1981, this is what eventually happened. My father had succeeded in obtaining a grant for completing his journalism studies and, as the political leadership for whom he had been working had changed in the meantime, he leapt on the opportunity to return to Europe.

The town of Neuhof in the southern suburbs of Strasbourg, where our family would unpack our bags once and for all, had only two black families; we would be the third. It was here we would experience a more precarious life, one of destitution and ostracism. Immigrants, especially their sons, know what it is like to be the butt of scathing remarks. But never could these ordeals strain the bond of body and soul that tied me to the Dark Continent. Although I had been born in Paris and, in the end, spent only four years living in the Congo—I have never gone back there—I have always felt close to Africa.

The "difficult" quarter—as it was described euphemistically—of Neuhof was the size of a small city. It extended over some 5,550 acres, upon which lived a multicultural mosaic of more than 20,000 inhabitants. Its vast green spaces and the village to which it was connected had less influence on its reputation than its conglomeration of HLM* projects. Some of the inhabitants found it amusing to read this acronym as an abbreviation for "Haut les mains!" because of the quarter's real or imagined lack of safety, its high unemployment rate, and the number of those living on public assistance (far higher than the national average). Also playing a role were the appalling record number of cars that were set on fire every Saint Sylvestre's Day [New Year's Eve] and the notorious criminal behavior exhibited by a certain marginal part of its population, which, although a minority, was quite active.

---

*[HLM is the acronym for habitation *à loyer moderé,* meaning "subsidized or low-rent housing." *Haut les mains* means "hands up." —Trans.]

We were given lodging in social housing, which was grouped together in endless towers and squat, barrack-like apartment buildings whose facades were constantly being renovated. Part of this housing was something called the Polygone, an unlikely hodgepodge of dilapidated shacks that had been allocated to a group of sedentary Gypsies. There we would regularly witness car chases in which the noisy rackets created by the roaring motors and squealing tires of stolen cars blended intimately with the wail of police sirens. Even then the funky hymns of Michael Jackson; Barry White; Kool & the Gang; Earth, Wind, and Fire; or Zapp spat out of speakers perched on windowsills and provided a sonorous backdrop to life in the quarter at all hours of the day and night. In Neuhof, the notion of disturbance of the peace had no currency or traction.

Our typical immigrant Congolese family—a well-read, overeducated father who was also a woman chaser; a mother devoted to her home; and their three young sons—found ourselves thus installed within a framework that continued to deteriorate year after year. My father, who graduated among the top of his class in political science, was what people call an "egghead." On several occasions he had been named to important positions, like advisor to the prime minister or star host of a televised news show on Congo Radio Television. It goes without saying that finding himself in this Strasbourg ghetto with the status of a simple student was not something he relished. According to what my mother says about it, he politely but firmly declined all offers of employment and saw to it that we were almost exclusively dependent on social assistance, a completely paradoxical attitude that he justified by stating that he refused to work under the authority of the white man. Thus it was my mother who shouldered the burden of head of the family as a result of this strange anticolonial militancy.

My father was a rare and refined individual. The milieu of notables to which his family belonged had endowed him with a good education and a sharp intelligence, and he was never caught dressed in less than his elegant best. Even in periods of want, he always dressed with extreme care and read books with improbable titles. I inherited his terrible beauty, which in his case sowed misfortune everywhere he went.

Upon our arrival in Strasbourg, I was placed in first grade before being dropped back to nursery school. I did not have the skill level required. In fact, I was so behind that the next year I had to repeat first grade because all the gaps in my education remained unfilled. But my father did not accept this dishonorable setback and made me work relentlessly for the entire summer. He subjected me to an extremely strict program, never once letting me play outdoors. Without letup, from morning to night, he had me working and revising to such an extent that the results were not long in coming. With this initiatory ordeal as my starting point, the course was set that would allow me to become and then remain a brilliant student. My father not only inculcated in me the absolute necessity of taking my studies seriously, but also gave me the ambition to be the best. Anything I gained this way, he told me, could never be taken away by anyone, and this treasure would be my greatest reward.

When my last brother, Stéphane, was born in 1983, my parents had already separated, and my father never saw his youngest son. As the song goes: "Papa was a rolling stone. . . ." Despite everything, I cannot help but feel affection toward this father-child. No doubt he also served me as an anti–role model, with his fickleness and libertine habits, whose consequences we suffered. But I have never been able to nurture the slightest feelings of bitterness toward him. When he left, my mother was all alone, with more than 50,000 francs worth of debt [approximately $10,000], no job, and four children in her charge; she did not receive any food assistance. On top of this, we were living in one of the worst neighborhoods of Strasbourg.

We had been doing better at the beginning. Mama, who had stayed sober until this point, now began drinking heavily. As with North American Indians and Australian Aborigines, alcohol seemingly offers some black Africans effective protection against everyday misery. Thus, the bottle becomes a reflex reaction of the peoples of these cultures when life's fortunes empty out; it drowns what is seen and thought in a cocoon of vapors. My mother, broken inside, took refuge in drinking heavily for many years. These were terrible years . . . but she never lost her dignity and never failed to do her best to raise us.

Of course, when we were children, it often happened that for several days at a stretch our three daily meals would all look like breakfast. And for Christmas and birthdays, we sometimes received toys bearing the stamp of the City of Strasbourg or that of Catholic Aid. The growing pile of unpaid bills sometimes forced us to resort to candlelight for a month, and hunger sometimes drove us to go through the door of Caritas to take advantage of its soup kitchen. But we were never ashamed. Mama herself was never ashamed. She told us that this was how our lives were supposed to unfurl, that this was our fate and we should accept it—without ever neglecting our prayers. For her the only sin was losing hope. Therefore, no matter what the weather—rain, wind, or snow, and even when she had her head completely fogged in by a colossal "post–Saturday African party hangover"—every Sunday she went to ask for help and mercy from Christ in the Church of Saint Christopher.

With the divorce of my parents, other families who had immigrated with them to the region scattered to points all over France, leaving us alone in Alsace. My mother refused to withdraw into herself and quickly wove solid ties with Maghreb, Turkish, Gypsy, and Alsatian families—ignoring all possible community divisions. Then numerous families from the Congo, and Zaire in particular, began arriving, and my mother made friends with a new crowd of drinking buddies, both men and women. This large African clan that formed around her gradually became our substitute family.

My mother had the natural temperament of a leader. The clear skin and fine features of this magnificent black woman contrasted with her great height and her imposing figure; she inspired fear even in the hearts of men. Because of this, she quickly imposed herself as the natural matriarch of this homesick community, and our modest apartment was never again empty of visitors. Against a background of Zairean rumba-rock by musicians like Franco, Tabu Ley, Lord Rochereau, Papa Wemba, or even the group Zaïko Langa-Langa, the matrons—whom we called *tantines*—were constantly busy preparing traditional dishes in the small kitchen on the edge of the explosion. I can still smell the aroma of *ponedou* (manioc leaf) tickling my nose, or that of *madessou* (white beans in sauce) accompanied by rice, semolina, and manioc that these matrons passed around while striding over cases of Kronenbourg or Kanterbrau strewn across the rooms of our small apartment.

In this tiny three-room apartment on the rue des Eyzies, my three brothers and I often slept in the same room. Frequently, we housed visiting cousins of both sexes, who would sleep in the canopy bed in the living room. There was obviously no room for a desk, and often I had to do my homework on a bed. This promiscuity did not disturb me excessively except when I was sick, and then I was given the privilege of taking refuge in my mother's room.

Our family moved three times, each time moving into a slightly larger apartment in Neuhof, thereby increasing our ability to host visitors. This perpetual African festival in which I lived until adolescence developed a tribal spirit in me as well as the distinct feature of talking loudly for no reason. It also left me with a profound aversion to alcohol, something that will stay with me, I think, for the rest of my life.

The lives of these expatriates from the Congo and Zaire swung between vice and virtue, between hope and resignation. For most of them, France was a kind of theater, a frozen stage on which they were barely actors. They were mere scraps of Africa, emptied of its spirit and set adrift. It was in the potting soil of the ghetto, feeding on this alienated culture, that I would grow up.

After Stéphane's birth and after my father's departure, it quickly became obvious that it would be in this quarter, where several communities— primarily Moroccan and Turk—cohabitated, that the fate of my family would unfurl. So, now far from her beloved Congo, my mother drew close to her host country. She wanted us to love this country because she knew we would never see hers again. She told me repeatedly that if I loved France sincerely, it could only love me back in return. "Opportunities can only be born in love," she also had a habit of telling me. No doubt she thought that through me she might be able to realize some of her own hopes. The fact remains that she never really talked to me in the same way that she talked to my brothers.

Her wise advice did not stop me from starting, at the age of eight or nine, to commit what are called *petite conneries* [little idiocies]. At first I was content just stealing candies from the corner aisle in the supermarket. This was, I have to say, a general habit widespread throughout the town. Then, with a handful of buddies, I graduated to small burglaries of apartments in the "bougie" part of the quarter, in Stockfled or the Ganzau. Oh, we did nothing truly heinous. We climbed the scaffoldings of the buildings under renovation and slipped through windows left partially open to pilfer baubles and other insignificant objects; we were even sometimes satisfied with just stealing the clothes that had been left to dry on the balconies.

This, however, was followed by the first gang muggings against other teenagers, most often young white boys from outside the neighborhood, which we did primarily for the sake of amusing ourselves on our way to the pool on Wednesdays or Saturdays. We would relieve these boys of their snacks, their personal effects, or—if we were in luck—their pocket money. Two or three times we even managed to force one of them to let us into his house to do a little plundering while his parents were away. New Year's Eve was invariably the opportunity to burgle the minimarkets of the neighborhood. With the help of small homemade bombs that were scarcely louder than the firecrackers and fireworks exploding all around us, we'd enter through back doors and fill our bags with all kinds of candy, chewing gum, and chocolate.

These activities were so common among the kids of the projects that no one saw any kind of real harm in any of it. But in my own case, it hardly fit in with my brilliant scholastic achievements. As it happens, one instructor, Miss Schaeffer—an octogenarian who hid a harsh face behind her huge, thick glasses and who lived only for the hope of see-ing us leave the ghetto through the door of learning—was absolutely convinced of my great potential. She badgered my mother about this as well, and she used all of her connections to get me accepted at the low-est cost to the Catholic private school, Saint Anne's, an elite establish-ment where hardly a single child from Neuhof had ever set foot.

It was thanks to her that I was able to gain access to another world outside that of the ghetto, and it was from this time that my contradic-tory activities began to become a real problem. Neither my classmates nor my mother could be allowed to get wind of the regular activities as a juvenile delinquent that I continued to perform in secret. It was imperative that I remain a model schoolboy and model son in their eyes. In this double life, I was lucky to have never been caught by the police (except for a completely harmless theft of some cassettes), and I had suc-cessfully completed the first part of my high school career keeping my justified but fragmentary reputation as an excellent student.

Few children in my neighborhood had benefited from this kind of opportunity, and even fewer in number were those who made something of it. Among the five hundred students attending Saint Anne's, Umit, who was of Turkish descent and who also lived in Neuhof, was the only one apart from me to be of foreign origin. But it was not because I was the only black and the poorest student in the school that I displayed such determination in my studies. I was not out for revenge; I simply loved school! My double life did not pose any moral conflict for me. It merely presented some practical problems surrounding my efforts to ensure I would not lose my image as a model student. My minor extra-curricular escapades, after all, were not something I viewed as "bad."

One of the professors who left the greatest impression on me was from my *classe de cinquième.** Mr. Leborgne was our English teacher, who also gave us religious instruction on Saturday morning. He spoke to us with as much communicative enthusiasm for Old Testament

---

*[The *classe de cinquième* is the equivalent of seventh grade in the United States. —*Trans.*]

prophets like Jeremiah as for the philosophers Voltaire or Alain. Each week he made us read and analyze extracts from the Bible, from *Propos sur l'education, Propos sur le Pouvoir,* or *Candide.** His harsh voice still echoes in my ears: "You must cultivate your garden. . . ." Using the full authority of his forty years, this large, strong, and hairy man adopted a strict air that was only emphasized by his thick black beard, which somehow made him seem more authoritarian to me.

His teaching methods conformed to his appearance as an English teacher. He stood for no nonsense, no chatter—not even a whisper—and seemed to delight in intimidating his students. After a well-placed verbal reprimand to one of his students, he couldn't hide the smile brought on by the sight of the boy bursting into tears. But this nasty austerity appeared to be a mere veneer that evaporated every Saturday when he unmasked his true self to us. I can still see him in his jogging suit with its Racing Club colors (often they were the same colors, which gave an impression that he owned several identical suits or that he hardly ever changed). He would stride back and forth across our large classroom with its blue varnished walls, while reciting almost by heart a passage from the Bible, such as Jeremiah 20:14–18, with the same gusto as a soccer fan:

> Cursed be the day wherein I was born! Let not the day wherein my mother bore me be blessed. Cursed be the man who brought tidings to my father saying: "A man child is born unto thee," making him very glad. . . . Wherefore came I forth out of the womb to see labor and sorrow, that my days should be consumed with shame.

This incongruous sight had a gripping effect on me. I had the

---

*[*Propos sur l'education* and *Propos sur le Pouvoir* (*Remarks on Education* and *Remarks on Power*) are works by French philosopher Alain (the pseudonym for Emile Chartier, 1868–1951); *Candide* is the best-known work by the French champion of the Enlightenment, Voltaire. —*Trans.*]

impression that he read these passages almost more for himself than for us, so greatly did his recital seem to transport him. Even those who were most insensitive to these lyrical fits of emotion appreciated his class for at least two reasons: it always involved one hour spent doing nothing but reading or listening and, most importantly, the class was held early Saturday morning and when it was over, our weekend officially began.

Around this time, I was beginning to realize the influence over others that my glib tongue and a certain imposing presence could give me—distinctions that I, of course, interpreted as indubitable signs of intelligence! It is certain that I distinguished myself easily both from my comrades of "the top" and the "young toughs" of the ghetto, who saw me as much more than just a "small fry" like them. This observation gave me an unshakable confidence in my abilities. My pride was partially rooted in my scholarly success and partially in the undeniable skills I was beginning to show evidence of—as a pickpocket.

I have no idea what triggered the phenomenon, but practically from one day to the next Neuhof became a breeding ground for pickpockets. All had more or less the same operating method; it was one that required three people to carry it off. The first person "picked" the wallet, whether it was in a purse or a pocket. The second person "blocked" the victim by attracting his attention and by doing something that made him stand still during the time it took to pull off the operation. And the third used his whole body as a screen to keep anyone from seeing the person who was doing the pick.

In mass transit or wherever people were jostling one another, this technique was so quick and nimble that the victims didn't notice a thing. There were, of course, neighborhoods particularly favorable for this kind of activity, namely tourist spots like the neighborhood surrounding the Strasbourg Cathedral, the Petite-France quarter, and generally speaking, the center of the city—provided there was a bit of a crowd. The German tourists who were imported there by the busload were our favorite prey. Contrary to the French, the Germans used neither checks nor credit cards and were always strolling around with wads of deutsch marks in their pockets.

On Saturdays we were treated to an influx of tourists, coupled with locals who had come to do their shopping with wallets full of cash; this was the best time of the week. Around thirty young pickpockets exercised their talents simultaneously, meticulously and discreetly covering the center of the city for the entire afternoon. The presence of plainclothes policemen prompted a certain caution, but nothing more than that. In any event, they were in the minority and therefore easily outnumbered, not to mention the fact that we were all minors and thus, at worst, we only risked being held overnight in police custody.

Therefore, every Saturday at eleven o'clock, after Mr. Leborgne's class and with my U.S. knapsack on my back, I would take the bus in the opposite direction of the one that would have brought me home. I was going "to work." My morning at school had brought me close to the center of the city, and the "open sesame" that was my bus pass allowed me to exercise my talents where the best customers were to be found. I would then meet up with Nouredine, who was nicknamed "Frog" because he hopped when he walked, and Toufik, known as "Handsome Kid" because the girls found him very attractive. I was certain to find them at the same place every week: in the back of the bus, rolling or smoking joints. These little trips would earn us between five hundred and a thousand francs each, sometimes more depending on our luck.

To be a pickpocket in my quarter was a consecration into the hierarchy of delinquency. During this period, except for a few isolated instances, the great stickup artists had not really appeared on the scene, especially because all of us were quite young. But valor does not depend upon age, and we all excelled in at least one discipline. I had already taken part in several burglaries, some shoplifting, and numerous violent thefts. Bikes and mopeds were often the objects of my desire because they were relatively easy to resell.

I was a member of a small band of crooks with three guys who were the same age as me: Majid, a pale boy with green eyes and brown hair; Khalid, who always peppered his speech with coarse language or salacious images; and Moussa, who had an enormous head and the fingers of a Turkish worker. I was particularly fond of the shy Majid, even if he had the annoying habit of spitting constantly. He even spit inside stores and malls, and it was almost necessary to restrain him from spitting in his own home! For some reason, he never spoke to anyone but me.

I no longer remember what our first scam was, but no doubt it was stealing cartons of cigarettes that we could resell individually on Sundays and holidays to the older guys hanging out in the street. By "older guys," we specifically meant all those who climbed "to work" in the city and who, for want of being in prison, had appeared at least once in juvenile court. We also frequently managed to pilfer bottles of whiskey from supermarkets outside the ghetto in order to resell them to the Vietnamese of our quarter, who were particularly fond of this type of alcohol. But for our activity to be profitable, we had to be inventive and multiply our schemes. This is how, equipped with jimmies, we robbed the cellars in certain bourgeois neighborhoods that we knew to be overflowing with bikes, scooters, and mopeds. After stealing two-wheelers with motors, we filed off their serial numbers; when it came to bicycles, all it took was a new paint job with a spray can and we were in business. When adding the proceeds from the resale of our take from the burglaries of apartments (which we specialized in), it's easy to see how I began earning quite a good living starting at the age of twelve.

During the week, we would all take the bus together to our respective schools. I was the only one still going to high school; the guys I hung out with went to a trade or technical school, where much of their time was spent as apprentices. In any case, the majority of them skipped their classes on a regular basis. We took over the entire back row of the bus, smoking Marlboros or Afghan hashish. I, however, did not consume either one, and I had enough self-confidence and legitimacy to give myself the luxury of declining my cronies' daily invitations to follow their example. "No, guys, I'm off to school. I only 'work' on weekends and during school vacations!" I'd say proudly, and everyone would burst out laughing. They were apparently impressed that I was able to tackle a private school education and maintain regular criminal activity at the same time. They did not confuse me with the "clowns" who thought success was only possible by slogging away at school, and who did not take advantage of the opportunities offered by life and who were forced to dress "like bums." The unusual combination of my persona—that of scam artist and respectable intellectual—attracted a certain friendliness toward me.

One Saturday, when I met up with Frog and Handsome, they were accompanied by Saïd, a black of Comorian origin who smoked joints while imitating the comical faces of Gainsbourg.* Saïd had just moved into our neighborhood. He was no choirboy and I knew it. I had met him one year earlier when he still lived in Meinau, another quarter, which was separated from ours by a large park.

It so happened that during this time, I was extorting a small white boy named Nicolas who also lived in Meinau and who had terrorized the bourgeois students of the high school before my arrival. Among other things, I had squeezed him for a nice Sony Walkman, which had belonged to this same Saïd. Unfortunately for me, Saïd and Nicolas's older brother were members of one of the most violent gangs of their neighborhood. Nicolas, seeing this as the opportunity to get his revenge on me, had mentioned Saïd to me while telling me to return the Walkman or face reprisals.

As a question of honor and principle, I refused to do so. This was why one day Saïd, who was at least four years my senior, was waiting for me with a friend at the door of Saint Anne's to teach me some basic lessons in generational respect. When they approached me, I gazed upon the face of Saïd for the first time. But when my glance met that of the guy accompanying him, we both cracked up laughing. It was Fat Rachid—also nick-named "Duck"—a neighbor who was also, incidentally, the best friend of

---

*[Serge Gainsbourg (1928–1991) was a very popular French poet, songwriter, actor, and director, whose funeral in 1991 virtually shut down the city of Paris. —*Trans.*]

my brother Arnaud. Thus, matters were quickly sorted out. I perceived luck as an inseparable quality of our being: having it or not defined us. This coincidence, which spared me a great deal of probable pain, helped to reinforce this conviction I held.

So, to return to the present moment of my story, on this particular Saturday Saïd was accompanying Frog and Handsome, who were waiting for me, just as they did every Saturday, to go "work" in the city center. Saïd sat down next to me and, with an amused smile, said: "I've come to break up your little ménage à trois, what d'ya think about that?" I grimaced and shrugged my shoulders as a sign of indifference. When we got to the square in front of the cathedral, populated as usual by numerous tourists, we came face to face with another three-man team already at work.

Among them was Nadir—the famous Nadir. I had known this small pale Algerian for a long time, but we had never worked together; he played in a higher division. He was just fifteen years old, barely two years older than me, but he was already a living legend: by himself he was making around fifteen thousand francs a day. Everyone called him "Golden Hand" because any purse he touched turned into a jackpot and somehow, inexplicably and luckily for him, he would never be free of that. Guys fought each other to work with him, but he never took more than two people into his crew. He made an exception for us that day, and I initially thought it was because he thought I was worthy.

Until then, Frog, Handsome, and I had been amateur snatchers of small pickings. However, with the honor Nadir bestowed upon us, we would become part of the gang, and this fact allowed us to enter a dangerous spiral. The excitement we felt was largely fueled by the very idea of that spiral. I would later learn from Saïd that he and Nadir had used our little group to muddy their trails: they had been followed for several days by plainclothesmen. Saïd also informed me that we had been swindled on every job that Saturday; Nadir had removed the greater part of the loot before the wallets had even been opened! My stupefaction was colored with admiration when I later learned from Nadir himself that he had also cheated Saïd even more readily, because this latter thought he was in his confidence.

My enjoyable education at Saint Anne's, which taught me how to best be a sensible youth, constructed an ideal of perfection for me. However, at the same time, I was living everyday life like a little Neuhof hoodlum. Thus was I constantly experiencing myself as my own opposite, the meeting place and frontier of two diametrically opposed worlds. It was only in the ivory tower of my personal awareness that I could attempt to recover my unity, and I did this by keeping reality at arm's length. For lack of being able to live otherwise, I continued to draw and quarter my ego by striving to evolve on two reversed hierarchies of values at the same time. I was a hoodlum more cunning than the rest, with a totally personal concept of spirituality. My kind of spirituality allowed to me to pray to God, not only for him to let me make more money, but also to not get caught by the police.

During my fourteenth year, I continued perfecting my pickpocketing technique, which, accompanied by Frog and Handsome Kid, was my primary activity. Handsome Kid had finally been baptized "Chemo" (verlan* for *moche* [ugly]) out of envy. With these two pals, I only worked in the city center, but at the same time I launched a "sideline job" by teaching myself how to deal drugs in the ghetto with Majid, Khalid, and Moussa. Moussa had a brother whose personal consumption of shit could have supported an entire armada of drug dealers. We took advantage of this situation to sneak two or three grams a week, just a drop in the ocean really, and cut this shit with a certain quantity of henna. We cooked and dried the mixture before reducing it into small balls that we then mixed with tobacco. The final result was put into small plastic bags and sold to kids our own age who had rarely or never smoked before.

This swindle prospered for several months, mainly thanks to one of the older guys in the ghetto who, after smoking our mixture, swore to whomever would listen that he had smoked the same thing in Jamaica.

*[Verlan is a form of slang that reverses the first and last syllables of a word. —*Trans.*]

I, meanwhile, told people—with so much confidence that no one would ever dream of doubting me—that the weed came from the Congo.

My thirst to learn was just as avid for these extracurricular disciplines as it was for my academic studies: after every new feat, I was ready to learn another. This was how, by seeking to extend the extent of my skills even further, I first felt Death's shadow loom over my adolescent horizon. I had already taken several rides in stolen cars and participated in the "hot-wiring" of an auto, but I did not know how to drive. It was therefore necessary for me to learn so that I could work alone. The example of car thieves in my neighborhood—who had all attained notoriety, if not posterity (several had died in the "performance" of their duties)—impelled me to follow in their footsteps.

This was the route I absolutely had to take if I wished to become a person of prestige. Hicham, who lived in the apartment building facing mine on rue des Eyzies—the heart of the trafficking in the neighborhood—had some experience with this and offered to teach me to drive. He also promised absolute discretion. But at the appointed time, he kept me waiting all afternoon in the stairwell of my building. When he finally showed up, he explained that he had been slogging the whole day before finding, in the pretty Petite-France quarter, a white 405 MI 16!

All at once, and I still do not know why, I no longer wanted to go with him. When I told him this, he insulted me and then took off alone. He would not be seen alive again. Later that day, zooming around in the stolen car, he attracted the attention of some motorcycle cops, who took off in pursuit of him. When motorcycle cops appear in a rearview mirror, the goose of the person they are chasing is generally cooked, except in films or legends. The few witnesses who saw the car chase reported that Hicham drove like a pro. But he could not avoid an accident, and when his car exploded, he no doubt died on the spot.

My lifestyle at this time was all show. I was typically clad in very expensive Fila or Ellesse jogging suits, and on my feet I wore the latest Nikes or Adidas, which cost more than 700 francs a pair. The jogging suits could not be gotten in France, but had to be purchased in Germany or Switzerland.

My cronies and I had gotten into the habit of hanging in a discotheque called Le Paradise, whose doors opened on Sunday afternoon. This club had the distinction of being frequented by the worst delinquents of the city: dealers, pickpockets, burglars, shoplifters, and purse snatchers from Neuhof, Elsau, Kronenbourg, Hautpierre, Kœnigshoffen, Meinau, and even the quarter in which the Strasbourg train station was located. Le Paradise was a den of thieves, and many deals went down there. Fortunes were spent on showing off, with everyone competing with bottles of champagne and whiskey, accompanied by girls that this kind of life excited.

Showing off: this was definitely the sole objective. It was necessary to show everyone that money was no longer a problem. Generosity was a sign of wealth. In restaurants, rounds of drinks were offered to the house, and numerous money orders were sent to cronies in prison. This latter was an obligation that was all the more respected because everyone was well aware that he could find himself in the same situation at any unpredictable moment.

There was nothing Robin Hood–like about our activities; concerns for social justice had absolutely no motivation for us. All of our illegal operations were conducted strictly for our own profit, and with dead seriousness we considered them our trade—the way we earned our daily bread. When one had a regular girlfriend, it was tradition to take her to an ultrachic restaurant on Friday evening, something like Le Petit Maxim or Le Crocodile, before spending the night in a hotel with her. On Saturday morning, one left "for work" until the end of the afternoon, then wisely went back to the hotel where the girl was generally waiting. Once night fell, one left for Charlie's, another fashionable club. The weekend ended at Le Paradise after which time the girl would be brought back home—in a taxi, it almost goes without saying.

I was able to follow this program only on school vacations, because even though I looked like I was eighteen, I was still, nonetheless, only a big, awkward fourteen-year-old lump of a boy. Furthermore, my financial margins were confined because the image I presented to my mother, that of an exemplary child, forced me to operate clandestinely. For example, I set a clothing budget for myself and would tell her that I shopped in the neighborhood where guys sold things at prices that beat all the competition: fifty francs for an article of clothing that might be worth a thousand! Of course, the sellers were obviously receiving stolen goods, but everybody, even my mother's friends, participated in this kind of activity in the quarter.

What bugged me the most about this state of affairs was being forced to ask my mother for pocket money that I had no need for at all. Seeing the astronomical sums that were flowing through my fingers, my older brother Arnaud threatened to reveal everything to her if I did not give him a hefty percentage. This blackmail went on for several years, but I was ready to meet his price so that my mother would maintain a good image of me.

In Neuhof, delinquency was not merely a lucrative activity, it was first and foremost a state of mind, and the absence of certain mental and moral attitudes it engendered was crippling. Owning a big mouth was of no use whatsoever, what mattered was efficiency. A friend who was a hold-up man and who lived on Schach Street told me a story that provides a good illustration of this principle. A guy from another neighborhood showed up in Neuhof one day after hearing that a stickup was being planned. He arrived like a prince, recommended by someone we trusted, and he never stopped bragging. To listen to him it was certain that once the action had gone down, his name would be on everyone's tongue.

But as the time of the action drew near, he became less and less voluble. On the appointed time and day, he fell apart completely. Hardly had our lascars left the car when the braggart crapped his pants, both figuratively and literally, if I may say so. In tears, he refused to move forward, and the others, scared that they would be detected, climbed back into the vehicle and roared off. Everything had been planned down to the smallest detail, but no one had figured on this kind of hitch. Several minutes later, his companions abandoned him, still sobbing, in the very middle of the main road. This had never happened to them before, and the neighborhood is still laughing about it today.

But the guy had finally succeeded in making a name for himself in Neuhof.

My generation still kept the memory of Jacques Mesrine alive. Mesrine was public enemy number one during the '60s. He had escaped from prison numerous times and was someone who, to us, represented a prince of high banditry, courtesy, and fair play. He was the ultimate reference point for the real delinquents of my quarter. Like him, they boasted an ethical standard formed of rigor, loyalty, courage, and most importantly, respect. This involved behaving like a "good guy," which meant being effective and discreet in both life and work. Those who stuck to this discipline were never worried and their plans never ended in costly screwups or a bloody settling of scores. When a difference of opinion separated them, they settled the matter man to man, with a bare-handed fistfight.

The police also obeyed this code. As long as they had nothing to hold against you and you behaved correctly, they would leave you alone. One day when we were out hanging around and a police wagon was patrolling at the crossroads, one of the older guys shouted: "Death to the pigs!" as the patrol wagon went by. It immediately braked to a complete stop.

Three policemen got out. "Who said that?" one of them yelled.

As no one moved a muscle, the patrolman acted as if he was about to turn away when one of the older guys yelled behind his back: "Without your badge and your gun, you wouldn't be acting so tough!"

Without a second's hesitation, the patrolman took off his helmet and his badge, and entrusted one of his colleagues with his gun. "C'mon then, let's settle this man to man. . . ."

The other accepted this challenge without hesitation, and the fight that ensued was relatively balanced. After several minutes, the policeman prevailed, but when the patrol wagon drove away there were no riots or stone throwing. A certain code of honor still reigned, and "respect" was the master word—respect for parents, elders, and especially the adults of the neighborhood. Just because someone was the worst kind of hoodlum did not give him the right to behave however he pleased. But all this would soon fall to pieces when the older guys, one after another, began falling into the hell of drugs.

As I said, I never smoked—even if I rolled joints for my buddies to amuse myself—and I drank very little. Everyone on the street knew that the worst elements in the business were those who were hooked on something. This is why I stayed clean and thereby kept a head start on the others. I learned this from observing Nadir Golden Hand. When drugs appeared in Neuhof, it was not long before there were real ravages in our ranks. Since the time I was seven or eight, I had seen the older guys getting high by sniffing packs of the extrastrong glue used to patch the tires of small two-wheelers. The glue quickly fell out of fashion, and everyone seriously began turning to shit and alcohol. Later, as a result of regular trips to Germany, Holland, and Switzerland "to work," but also to have a good time (mainly with prostitutes), many people eventually started returning with heroin in their baggage to prolong the pleasure. . . . This really took off, like a trail of gunpowder, if I can describe it that way.

Fat Rachid—who had not been my brother's best friend for a long time—had gotten into the habit of coming over between noon and two so that we could take the bus together to school. His school was located six stops past mine. One day, he had something he absolutely had to show me before we got on the bus. He took me into a cellar of his apartment building. All those individuals I had run into when I worked in the center of the city were there, with the exception of Majid, Khalid, Moussa, and Nadir, and they were all in the process of snorting dope. Because of the energy they exhibited afterward, I imagine it was cocaine.

I was stunned because until then, except for rumors in my entourage to the contrary, everyone denied ever touching what they called "death." If initially cocaine was used, it was only a matter of time before the user graduated to heroin, which was much more harmful, mentally and physically, than cocaine. Everyone gained entrance to the vice of heroin through the door of cocaine. This was the real tragedy. The older guys had been the first affected for two reasons: their constant trips to Holland and, more importantly, as a result of having seen the film *Scarface*.

The hero of this film, Tony Montana (brilliantly acted by Al Pacino), is a Cuban immigrant refugee in the United States who starts off as a small-time dealer before reaching the top of the pyramid of crime—while putting all the cocaine in the country up his nose in the meantime. Now forgotten was the worthy Mesrine, who had been our idol. It was terrifying to see to what extent Tony Montana became the absolute model for many of the guys in the poor neighborhoods. Some even knew all his lines by heart! This phenomenon scared me. I could not understand how a simple film could give birth to so much destruction. Convinced that I, too, ran a risk of succumbing to this morbid fascination, I found every excuse to avoid seeing *Scarface*, whereas some of my buddies saw it eight or nine times. (I only saw this masterpiece much later.)

The case of *Scarface* is particularly extreme, but the cinema generally had a certain influence over our behavior—the way we reasoned and everything that formed our values and imagination. Among the most significant films, we can undoubtedly include the work *Boyz 'n the Hood,* by the black American director John Singleton. This film, which paints a picture of the tragic everyday life in one of the most dangerous black ghettos of Los Angeles, stars the famous rapper and actor Ice Cube. *New Jack City,* with the famous black actor Wesley Snipes, created a New York version of *Scarface*.

If we leave out hip-hop films like *Beat Street* or the two parts of *Breakstreet* and Spike Lee's *Malcolm X,* the cinema had a completely negative effect on us. It goes without saying that our aspirations and daily lives corresponded exclusively to the lifestyles of the "bad guys." For want of upstanding role models, we absolutely did not have the maturity necessary to put distance between ourselves and these characters, each more charismatic than the last. And if they died at the end, we thought it was specifically because we were watching a film; this wasn't real life!

In real life, *we* were the ones who played those roles, and up until the present, we had always won. It seemed to us that we had the world at our feet for all of eternity, and we treated everyone who did not agree like clowns. *Scarface* fit into this tendency; it was *the* film that adjusted perfectly to this mania.

The majority of the guys I saw snorting dope that day in that cellar are now dead. Some of them died of AIDS, but the majority died of overdoses. The story of Abd al Slam is a great illustration of the surreal situations to which hard drugs gave birth. He lived in the same building as I did, and one day, from my kitchen window, I watched him pass by. He was returning home from a detoxification center where he had spent the past several months. He looked relatively together as he disappeared in his stairwell, and this idea gave me some comfort when my mother sent me to pick some items up at the minimarket for her.

On my return, an ambulance, a patrol wagon, and a number of curious onlookers were blocking the door to my building. I threaded my way into the crowd, asking what was going on. It seems that Abd al Slam, just out of detox, had hidden in the local bike shop in order to shoot up a dose of heroin—a dose that was too strong. He was the first in the neighborhood to die in this fashion. Unfortunately, many others soon followed in his footsteps. The famous afternoon in the cellar and numerous tragedies like that of Abd al Slam left their mark on me. It became harder and harder to put together a team of guys who wouldn't touch the stuff. The situation grew worse by the day, with similar tragedies becoming commonplace.

One evening, Frog, Chemo, and I decided to go to a nightclub that normally refused to let us in. A certain Babine—nicknamed that because he always sputtered when he talked, but especially because he had enormous lips—had been able to gain entrance there and offered to go with us on the condition that we make a one- or two-hour detour to visit his sister, whom he had not seen for several weeks.

The neighborhood was pleasant, the apartment cute, and the person who opened the door upon our knock was the sister's boyfriend. They were apparently just finishing dinner; a kid of about three or four years old was running all over the place and called Babine *tonton* [uncle]. A guy was sitting on the sofa smoking a cigarette. Hardly several minutes after our arrival, we were offered a very special aperitif: on a small silver tray were lines of brown heroin that had been prepared to celebrate the birthday of the boyfriend. Everyone, including Frog and Chemo, indulged themselves wholeheartedly in front of the kid, who must have, in all likelihood, witnessed this kind of scene regularly.

I was disgusted. The guy on the sofa insisted that I take a snort with them, which I pretended to do so that he would leave me alone. I implied that I had already gotten "loaded" before coming over. Around the break of dawn, the party finally came to an end, without us ever managing to have gotten out of the apartment. I left the living room in silence; everyone was sleeping, sprawled all over, stiff and high. I wondered how I had been able to watch their drug-addicted delirium all evening without slamming the door in their faces. While climbing the stairs of my building, I swore never again to hang with anyone doing drugs. I decided to cloister myself in my room for several weeks once classes ended and to carefully avoid hanging around with anyone from the neighborhood. This reclusive period, which lasted until I was down to my last penny and forced to go back "to work," allowed me to reflect on my situation.

I had felt an immediate aversion to drugs. On the one hand, I considered any form of dependence a sign of weakness, and on the other hand, I was terrified at the idea that once I went down that path it would be impossible for me to turn back. Frog and Chemo's descent into hell confirmed this notion. I knew them well enough to know that they had minds of tempered steel, and it appeared totally impossible, despite all of their faults, that they could become drug addicts. I had always sought to mark myself off from the gray crowd of the ghetto, which motivated me to persevere on the path of moderation, if not outright abstinence, from alcohol and shit.

There are, of course, individuals who smoke shit without ever falling into addiction to the hard stuff. But in fact, consumers come in two varieties. Some smoke shit to entertain themselves or as a display of their "refusal of the system"—but these individuals are rare. Except for the organizers of social and cultural centers, the Marxist revolutionary type who wears a keffiyeh like a scarf, I have to confess that I never knew any. The others, the majority by far, smoked to fill an inner emptiness and inevitably buried themselves deeper in the activity of getting high. They started by drinking, passed almost immediately over to shit, and were certain to find themselves confronted by dope soon thereafter. Their need for strong sensations was rooted in social poverty, and they veiled it with smoke. But this veil would always dissipate far too quickly, and they were forced to go further and further to achieve the release they were looking for. However, during the time one is stoned, one's wretched situation has not stopped growing worse . . . quite the contrary.

The drug addicts multiplying in this compost were of the worst kind and no longer recognized any kind of principle. They would even beat up their own mothers for a bank note, and when they "worked" they had no concern for anything, therefore putting their colleagues in grave peril for a quarter gram of heroin. Over the course of time, if they didn't OD in the meantime, they were often recruited as snitches by the RG.* In the ghetto, even those who did not fall into hard stuff entered this unhealthy spiral by making themselves "sellers of death," dealers of hard drugs.

It was in the midst of this chaos that the current generation was

---

*[The RG is the *renseignement generaux,* the intelligence division of the French police, created by the Vichy government of Pétain during World War II for political spying. —*Trans.*]

born, who, because of the older generation's predilection for drugs, found themselves left to their own devices. The people who should have been role models had become either derelicts shooting up from morning to night or else lawless, faithless dealers who would betray their own fathers and mothers for a few francs. How could anyone have respect for people like this? Guys found themselves doing business with kids who were ten or even fifteen years younger than they were, while others allowed themselves to be physically and verbally assaulted by gangs of kids no older than their own children.

The new generation of policemen, overwhelmed by this gratuitous violence and hatred, and sometimes recruited from the same criminal breeding grounds, often responded with a brutality that was both blind and disproportionate. This excuses nothing concerning the attitude of the young in question, but it explains a lot: the sole lasting consequence of this unleashed violence was to make the young crazy with rage against a society that entrusted such decadent men with keeping order.

Arnaud resembled our father greatly, especially physically. His skin was much darker than mine, but his nose and mouth were finely formed, and he never said much. He was well known throughout the neighborhood because he too had had a momentous childhood: every Saturday the police brought him home because of various and diverse thefts, and every Saturday he invariably received the thrashing of the century from our mother.

As a kid, Arnaud did an enormous number of stupid things, which was almost pathological, and my mother, who was still vigorous during this time, tried time and again to give him memorable—but ineffective—corrections. However, in the space of a day, he ceased all criminal activity, for two reasons that are a priori diametrically opposed. First, he told me how, one evening, he was awoken by a strange glow above his bed. He swore to me that he was perfectly awake when he saw a black man dressed in white, floating barefoot above his bed; this man asked him to embrace Islam.

Now, while I believe that Arnaud embellished the telling of this disturbing vision a little, the fact remains that dating from this day he abstained from eating pork and began fasting every year during the month of Ramadan. I then shared my room with him, and during the several weeks of respite that I gave myself after the famous night when my three buddies shot up, I was particularly sensitive to the speech my brother made to me every evening about the veracity of the mission of the last of the prophets. In tandem, he had discovered the company of the female sex, and these apparently contrary forces, Islam and girls, removed him, once and for all, from the chaos of the street.

As for me, after a time of retreat, it became imperative that I "make myself over." I was keenly aware that the legitimacy I had acquired in the street would deflate like a balloon if I had empty pockets. But as I no longer wished to travel in the company of druggies, and because Majid had cut me off cold because I had not put him onto any scams for several months, and because I had broken with Moussa for the same reasons and had lost track of Khalid, I found myself urgently in need of a new teammate. This was how I began to spend time with a certain Mohammed. "Glue Pot" was initially a buffoon, a completely clueless individual who understood nothing about anything and who, if one showed him any sympathy, did not want to let go.

Everyone avoided him like the plague, and as a result, he had gotten into the habit of "working" solo, and he eventually became quite good at it. Most importantly, he neither smoked nor drank, nor did he take drugs. His specialty was snatching purses. One Wednesday afternoon, Glue Pot took me with him to scout around. The street we arrived at was located in front of my high school, next to the Church of Saint Aloysius, and this was a coincidence that I did not know how to interpret.

He explained to me that the old ladies who passed that way often carried princely sums of money in their handbags. Rarely did I pick the elderly to be my victims, and on those few occasions when I had, I showed evidence of a certain deftness and delicacy, if I may say so myself. So we got down to work. We quickly found ourselves close on the heels of an old woman whose elegance seemingly foretold a fortune. After discreetly following her into a tiny, isolated street, we decided to take action. The plan was simple: Glue Pot was supposed to dash by and snatch her handbag while I ran right behind him to grab it in the event he let go or snatch it myself if he missed his chance. This was the double-edged-razor principle: dual action for more security.

But events did not transpire in practice as foreseen in the imagination. Neither Glue Pot nor the woman would let go of the purse, and she collapsed on the sidewalk from the violent shock of his assault. Glue Pot dragged her over the pavement for more than six feet while I yelled at him to let go of the blasted purse, but he ignored me, and after a few seconds it was she who ended up letting go. During this entire time—an eternity—and despite the surprise and brutality of her assailant, she made not a cry, not even the slightest groan.

I felt dirty.

Leaving the old woman on the ground, we began running at full speed without once looking back, until we got home to the neighborhood. The irony of this entire story is that the purse did not even contain twenty francs—but it would still have been a sordid and inexcusable story if this had *not* been the case. I didn't see Glue Pot again until many years later when I ran into him on Place Kléber, entirely stupefied by alcohol. With a bottle of whiskey in his right hand, he swore to me with the other that it had been months since he had touched a drop.

This incident with Glue Pot and the old lady traumatized me and radically forced me to repossess my life. Even today, I am still haunted by the image of that woman falling down silently before me. For a period of several weeks, I scrupulously read the news in a brief column in the *Dernières Nouvelles d'Alsace,* but they never mentioned it. Perhaps it was too commonplace.

Many of my acquaintances lived this life to the point of absurdity. They are either dead or have gone mad. I lived on the other side of the mirror and came back. It is the duty of each of us to give our testimony. . . .

J'ai tout appris a l'école de la rue, mes profs les ennuis
J'ai compris qu'il fallait que je change toute ma vie
Il ne suffit pas d'avoir la bonne porte, il faut the bonne
*   clef*
Se remettre en question, se dire maintenant j'dois changer
J'en ai assez de vivre comme ça depuis qu't'es plus là
J'ai tout perdu, plus rien sera plus comme autrefois
I' faut pas oublier les siens, les nôtres qui disparaissent
Ce sont des signes clairs, l'existence est comme un test
Un examen d'passage, passagèrement t'es mis en avant
On agirait pas comme ça si on savait c'qui nous
*   attend. . . .**

Translation:

I learned everything in the school of the street, trouble
    was my teacher
I realized I had to change my whole life
It is not enough to have the right door; it requires the
    right key
Challenging yourself, telling yourself now I should
    change
I've had enough of living like this now that you are no
    longer here
I've lost everything, nothing can be like it was before
We should not forget our own, our people who have
    died
For these are clear signs; life is like a test
An exam to pass, temporarily you get put in front
We would not act this way if we knew what was in
    store for us. . . .

---

*NAP [New African Poets], *"Au revoir à jamais"* ["Good-bye Forever"], extract from the album *La fin du monde* [The End of the World], Editions Chrysalis Music, France.

TO THE MEMORY OF

Abd al Slam	Overdose
Alain	Car accident
Christophe	Aneurysm
David	Murdered
Djamel	Murdered
Djean Pes	Overdose
Fabien	Motorcycle accident
Farouk	AIDS
Fouad	Murdered
Galem	Accident
Hamedi	Suicide in jail
Henri	Overdose
Jean-Pierre	Car accident
Joël	Car accident
Manu	Motorcycle accident
Nadège	Overdose
Papy	Murdered
Rachid	Overdose
Slim	Murdered
Yann	Overdose

And to all the others, may they rest in peace. . . .

TWO

||||||||||||||||||||||||||||||||||||||||||||

THE MUSTARD SEED

A person imprisons himself in a role and the other
  becomes too much, no?
And I suppose this takes one even farther from oneself
Nonlove is a tragedy I am the first to ask for help
I want to be wise as Heraclitus, because it smells more like
  gunpowder everywhere
We have the same blood that runs red, no matter what
  idea or principle
Find another ethical more positive skin brother don't
  forget that time is pressing
Before the end comes we really need to be united
Otherwise people will be tearing each other to pieces, they
  will be fighting each Other
                    From the song "Allah Bless France"

At the end of every trimester, the director of the Saint Anne High School, Madame Nassau, did us the signal honor of announcing our school grades to us in person, which provided the basis for a complete ceremony. (Her facial features were irresistibly reminiscent of François Mitterand, though it must be said that she had almost as much power over us as the man the media dubbed "God.") Her visit was impromptu; no one, apparently not even the teachers, ever knew in advance either the hour or what class she would choose to visit. So the excitement with which we rose from our seats was all the greater once she opened the door without knocking. With an affected air, and after having looked us up and down for what seemed an eternity but must have lasted only a few seconds, she invited us to resume our seats as if she were granting us a huge favor. Then, at the call of our name, each student, trembling over a dismal sea of bowed heads, arose to be either praised or decapitated by Madame the Director.

I had been particularly brilliant over this final trimester of eighth grade. It should be noted that the stakes involved were quite high: my success would not only give me access to high school, but also to the essential grant that would cover the costs of my continued education. I was planning, once I had put middle school behind me, to enroll in Notre Dame des Mineurs, a private Catholic school that was one of the best secondary schools of Strasbourg.

My mother's joy when I announced the news of my success was such that she organized a party equal to the event. "My son is going into ninth grade . . . at Notre Dame!" she exclaimed while embracing me and weeping. This victory had an exceptional value. By way of contrast, my brother Arnaud—who everyone called Bilal since his conversion to Islam—had been directed to vocational school since sixth grade, as were the majority of kids living in the ghetto. There was nothing shameful about this in and of itself, but it did tangibly reduce one's future prospects—which in our context meant rendering them practically null.

I have to say that after the episode with the old woman and the handbag, I had plunged into my studies with renewed enthusiasm. My new playmates were named Seneca, (Albert) Camus, Epicetes, (George) Orwell, (Aimé) Césaire, Thucydidus, (Frantz) Fanon, Saint Augustine, (René) Barjavel, (Aldous) Huxley, or Cheikh Anta Diop. I was particularly affected by anything that dealt with the history and culture of black people in general. I recall reading Alex Haley's *Roots* in a single day and then weeping the entire night over the tragic fate of Kunta Kinte and all the blacks of America. These heroic figures fascinated me; their entire beings were engaged in a struggle that awoke a profound echo in me. They became the tutelary figures of my life, giving it meaning and carrying me toward a new horizon. And as I conversed with them, I had the impression of expanding into an entirely new dimension because I suddenly found myself filled with the irrepressible desire to leave my world and to go beyond my own forces.

But it was Malcolm X, the black American Muslim leader who was a pacifist but who challenged nonviolence, who made the deepest impression on me. At the university library where I had gotten into the habit of studying, I made the acquaintance of Thierry, a large blond with an Alsatian accent who was studying anthropology and whose mind was completely fixed on Africa—something I could not help but find comic. He pulled off the feat of procuring for me a photocopy of the entire *Autobiography of Malcolm X,* which included several of the final speeches that Malcolm X had given in 1965, the year of his death.

I learned that my hero was born in 1925 in Omaha, Nebraska, of a pastor father who was murdered by the Ku Klux Klan and a mother who was completely destroyed psychologically (and who had to be institutionalized) after this tragic event. Malcolm X lived first in Boston, then New York, cities in which he was a burglar and a dealer in turn. He spent seven years in prison for these various crimes and became a "black Muslim," which is to say a member of the Nation of Islam, a black separatist movement founded and directed by Elijah Muhammed, who was freely inspired by the Muslim faith. Once released from prison, Malcolm X rapidly imposed himself as the charismatic figure of this movement and gave it a national scope.

By centering the activity of the Nation of Islam on the struggle for civil rights, he also made himself the champion of the underprivileged blacks of the United States. His impassioned diatribes against the system implemented by the whites and his invectives against those he nicknamed "Uncle Toms"—those blacks whom he considered to be vassals of the whites and traitors to their race—made him a leader whom the media soon set up as the opposite of Martin Luther King Jr., whose nonviolent approach he challenged.

Following several journeys through Europe, Africa, and the Middle East, but especially after his conversion to orthodox Islam, he broke relations once and for all with the Nation of Islam and the racist rhetoric it espoused. From Saudi Arabia, where he was then making a pilgrimage to Mecca, he wrote an unforgettable letter to his family and his friends, who hastened to distribute it to the media. My entire being throbbed with exaltation when I discovered this letter, and I read and reread it at least a hundred times. It represented such a turning point in my directionless adolescence that I want to give a sample of its tone here:

Never have I witnessed such sincere hospitality and the overwhelming spirit of true brotherhood as is practiced by people of all colors and races here in this Ancient Holy Land, the home of Abraham, Muhammad, and all the other prophets of the Holy Scriptures. For the past week, I have been utterly speechless and spellbound by the graciousness I see displayed all around me by people of all colors.

America needs to understand Islam, because this is the one religion that erases from its society the race problem. . . . You may be shocked by these words coming from me. But on this pilgrimage, what I have seen and experienced has forced me to re-arrange much of my thought patterns previously held, and to toss aside some of my previous conclusions. . . .

During the past eleven days here in the Muslim world, I have eaten from the same plate, drunk from the same glass, and slept in the same bed (or on the same rug)—while praying to the same God—with fellow Muslims, whose eyes were the bluest of blue, whose hair was the blondest of blonde, and whose skin was the whitest of white. And in the words and in the *actions* and in the *deeds* of the "white" Muslims, I felt the same sincerity that I felt among the black African Muslims of Nigeria, Sudan, and Ghana.

We were *truly* all the same (brothers)—because their belief in one God had removed all the "white" from their *minds,* the "white" from their *behavior,* and the "white" from their *attitude.*

I could see from this, that perhaps if white Americans could accept the Oneness of God, then perhaps, too, they could accept *in reality* the Oneness of Man—and cease to measure, and hinder, and harm others in terms of their "differences" in color.

With racism plaguing white America like an incurable cancer, the so-called "Christian" white American heart should be more receptive to a proven solution to such a destructive problem. Perhaps it could be in time to save America from imminent disaster—the same destruction brought upon Germany by racism that eventually destroyed the Germans themselves.

And he signed his letter with his Muslim name: El Hadj Malik el-Shabazz.

Upon his return to the United States, he proposed to register a formal complaint at the United Nations against America for its racist, violent, and segregationist policies. He also proposed joining with Martin Luther King Jr. and all the leaders of good will—blacks and whites— who wished to fight together for equal rights. But on Sunday, February 21, 1965, he was struck down by sixteen bullets from a revolver, during a meeting in Harlem. He was thirty-nine years old.

I was fascinated by this destiny and steeped myself in the final message of a man who had succeeded in surpassing the stage of resentment to enter into one of universal struggle. With these photocopies, I was plunged into a veritable voluntary exile of reading and introspection, and I began to assess the weight of my actions. For me, up until that time, the distinction between good and evil was very fuzzy: it was a question of discerning "what did one good" in the egotistical sense, or what did not. This subtle distinction is an important one; the entire mentality of my neighborhood was built around it. But with the specter of drugs, which lurked all around me with the deaths they claimed, and with the image of that woman knocked down to the ground still pursuing me, the street no longer shone for me as it once had. I was still living on it, of course, but it no longer had the same attraction for me. My heart was no longer in it, and I felt like a prisoner there. My heart had thrilled to the call of Malcolm X and now needed something different.

My mother had renewed ties with my paternal aunt after her husband had abandoned the conjugal hearth, leaving her with the responsibility of their three children: Frédéric, the eldest, who wore large brown eyeglasses that were at least trifocal; Laurence, who was scared stiff of dogs; and Muriel, who was still a chubby-cheeked baby. We spent our vacation in Paris that year, at the home of this aunt. During our stay, my cousin Frédéric introduced me to French rap music, which was just emerging.

Bilal and I were already familiar with American rap, but we did not believe it existed in France until our cousin made us listen to Radio Nova, where NTM and MC Solaar, among others, got their starts. Upon our return from Paris, Bilal decided to form his own rap group. He spoke to his three best friends who shared the same passion for music: Mustapha, Majid's elder brother, who had a terribly cut Afro and incredible dentition; Karim, who never stopped talking; and Mohammed, the oldest of the trio, a long, thin guy who opened his mouth only to tell jokes that he alone understood. The four of them formed the New African Poets (NAP). Majid and I got into the habit of attending the first rehearsals of the group, which took place in the neighborhood's multipurpose center. It was this that finally gave us the opportunity to reconcile. My time hanging in the neighborhood had been reduced to almost nothing, so I awaited these Wednesdays with real impatience.

It would probably be a good idea for me to stop here to explain to the ignorant—I am joking, of course—what rap and hip-hop culture represent.

Let's start with a little history. Rap, a kind of talking song spoken to a beat, first appeared in the New York ghetto at the beginning of the 1970s. Some even trace it back to the Last Poets, because this black American group from the East Coast was the first to employ its recitative technique. The musical support for their phrasing consisted almost exclusively of African percussion, djemba, and drum, with reference to the griots. In their Afrocentric texts, they preached a cultural and spiritual return to Africa, somewhat along the lines of Marcus Garvey, the "prophet" of the Rastafarians during the 1920s. The Last Poets, deeply imbued by the political vision of the Black Panthers, and in the example of Malcolm X, converted to Islam partially as an act of defiance against the white and racist American culture of that time. Some of them, namely the leader of the group, even finally left the United States. They settled for a while in France, and our paths sometimes happened to pass at the mosque on rue Tanger in the nineteenth arrondissement of Paris.

What gives rap its modernity is first and foremost its musical structure: melodic phrases extracted from other records and played in loops—the famous samples—on which a scratch is placed; scratches are the noises produced by the disc jockey (only later would they be called DJs) by manipulating the vinyl disks on the turntables. But the value and singularity of rap stem especially from its poetic texts, which carry messages of social protest. It was the group Grandmaster Flash and the Furious Five who gave this formula its popularity at the very beginning of the 1980s with the first rap hymn of the ghetto: "The Message," performed by Melle Mel.

Before this success there had been, and still are today, more festive and less antiestablishment rap titles performed by artists like Sugarhill Gang or Kurtis Blow—all from the East Coast. Songs from this neighboring genre sometimes rose to the tops of the American charts, but they were more similar to disco than to rap. "The Message," a dark and truly nihilistic title recounting ghetto life, was released over the airwaves for the first time and met with enormous success.

To channel this creative effervescence that had brought the Bronx to the boiling point, and to offer young people an alternative to endemic gang violence, the New York rapper Afrika Bambaataa had the idea of creating Zulu Nation, with reference to the fighting and resistant spirit of the Zulu people as embodied by, among others, Chaka, the founder of the Zulu empire in the eighteenth century. Initially, the goal of Zulu Nation was to structure and codify hip-hop as a multidisciplinary art movement, joining rap, dance (break dancing, smurf, and so on), DJ-ing (the art of scratching), and graffiti art (which spans the gamut from tag signatures in the street to wall murals painted with spray cans). It continued to maintain the cohesion of this movement around a pacifist and nonviolent mentality. This is why the charter of this movement was given the slogan "Peace, Love, Unity (and Havin' Fun)."

Hip-hop, a movement that was originally deeply rooted in black American culture, was able to cross the Atlantic and establish itself in Europe, particularly in France, for two very good reasons. Initially, it was hip, young Parisians who introduced it there and branded it as stylish, under such unexpected patronage as that provided by postpunk East German singer Nina Hagen and the couturier Paco Rabane. It is interesting to note that it was "young whites," as well as numerous Jews (Brooklyn is not far from the Bronx) that introduced to Paris a music whose mentors—Malcolm X, the Black Panthers, and even the former boxer Muhammed Ali—spent all their lives in diametrical opposition to the mentality and culture of white America. It is true that this antiestablishment aspect does not apply to all hip-hop, which has its festive, innovative, young, and pacifist sides as embodied by Zulu Nation, and which, without reference to any social origin, was the one that initially seduced a fringe group of Parisian youth before setting down much deeper roots.

Laurence Touitou is a figure who is a perfect representative of this movement. It was she, in fact, who produced the first show to offer a greater visibility to this culture, the show that went on to draw a cult following: *H.I.P-H.O.P.* Hosted by the rapper and dancer Sidney, and airing Sundays on channel TF1, this short program—barely half an hour long—adopted as its mission the initiation of its young viewers to the hip-hop movement by means of break dancing and smurf. It enjoyed phenomenal success in the poor neighborhoods, whose inhabitants felt orphaned when it was taken off the air sometime later.

Still as impassioned as ever, Touitou then founded, on the ashes of the first musical rap label in France (Label Noir), the first true house of rap records, Delabel. It was she who signed the Marseilles rappers of IAM and the singer Tonton David, among others. She also opened the doors to other musical genres by producing Rita Mitsouko and even the English musicians of Massive Attack (pioneers of what would later be called trip-hop, a kind of "trippy" technoid instrumental version of hip-hop).

During the period between the cancellation of the show *H.I.P.-H.O.P.* and the creation of Delabel, the other aspects of hip-hop (dance and, to a lesser degree, graphic work) were marginalized, to the benefit of its only musical part, rap. Groups like the Parisians of Assassin were precursors because they were among the first to rap in French, not contenting themselves with simply imitating the American model. This group, originally consisting of DJ Clyde and the two rappers Rockin' Squat and Solo, later developed a militant and anticapitalist form of rap. Parisian radio stations started appearing, like Radio 7, but most prominent was Radio Nova with Lionel D., its host and rapper. Franco-Algerian by birth, he lived in Vitry-sur-Seine in the southeastern suburbs, which contributed to amplifying the phenomenon.

During this time, Zulu Nation was being wrongly regarded as being part of the gangs of African immigrants who dedicated their efforts to all kinds of violence and trafficking, especially in the neighborhood surrounding the Forum des Halles.* Paradoxically, the media coverage of these criminal rackets, although condemned by the newscasters, greatly helped to popularize rap.

It is important to keep in mind that all these modes of expression emerged, initially, within a new generation of black Americans who could no longer identify with symbols of the past like Martin Luther King Jr. and the Black Panthers. Their need to assert their own identity in the face of the dominant white model manifested itself among the movement's precursors, if not by systematic conversion, at least by a feeling of sympathy for the Muslim religion. Not only was this a gesture of opposition to a specific American WASP culture, but they also had the feeling that this drew them closer to their African roots.

This is why, even before rap began to serve as a vehicle for this phenomenon, numerous North Africans living in the projects in France recognized themselves in such heroic figures as Muhammed Ali because of the fact they shared the same faith. This way of looking at things grew to such size that in Neuhof, when I was seven or eight years old, I often was told by Algerians or Moroccans hardly any older than me that Muhammed Ali was not truly black nor even truly American, otherwise how could one explain the fact that he was a Muslim? Some even went so far as to swear that he had been born in southern Algeria and emigrated to the United States with his family when he was still a child. But the young Moroccans did not share this opinion whatsoever: they were absolutely convinced that Muhammed Ali was in reality a Gnawa born in the region of Essaourira.

The form of Islam adopted by black Americans was quite far, however, from the religion that was practiced in the hinterlands of North Africa . . . when it was not strongly heterodox in the image of the Nation of Islam reconstructed by the racist Farrakhan. Whatever the case might be, this phenomenon of fusion (or confusion) constituted

---

*[The Forum des Halles is the large shopping mall complex that replaced what was once the huge food market in central Paris. —*Trans.*]

one of the factors for the rapid adoption of hip-hop and especially rap in the poor neighborhoods with North African majorities. In return, it also helped make Islam attractive to its young fans, whereas this religion had formerly been identified with their parents' generation, their values, and their history.

(American) rap was Muslim, as demonstrated by the examples of Big Daddy Kane, Rakim, and Special Ed. Later, *Malcolm X,* the cult film by Spike Lee, recounted the life of the black Muslim leader, as played by Denzel Washington (the black American actor par excellence, along with Morgan Freeman, not overlooking their precursor Sidney Poitier). This film definitively anchored the seductive figure of a cultural Islam among the population of the projects permeated by hip-hop culture, even if it was not a product of a Muslim culture.

It was thus in this context, between the cancellation of the *H.I.P-H.O.P* show and the first signings of rappers with a record label, that Bilal and the others founded NAP. During their first rehearsals, the group stuck to covers of songs by Parisian rappers like the Vitriots of the Little or the Sarcellois of Ministère Amer. Our cousin Frédéric was responsible for supplying Bilal with cassettes of Parisian rap that he recorded off Radio Nova. No other support was available during this period, as none of these artists had yet released a record. Finally, after seeing how Majid and I were faithful attendees of every rehearsal and how we were constantly negotiating over the telephone with Frédéric to send the latest freestyles (improvisations) from Nova, Bilal and the others offered to let us join the group. One of the great advantages of rap was how it broke free from the rigid guitar, bass, and percussion format in which rock was imprisoned; it offered much more adjustable group structures.

Our source of inspiration was Neuhof, because in contrast with our idols of the time, we did not live in the Parisian region. Like them, our motivation was not only art for art's sake, but also the need to give a voice to the projects. In Paris, the B. boys (a term designating the male members of the hip-hop movement—B. girls for females) would go flaunt themselves at the Globo, a trendy hip-hop club that was all the rage, or snort their first lines of coke at bourgeois soirées. We, meanwhile, were still squatting at the foot of our public housing units, an ever-so-fulfilling occupation from which we sometimes tore ourselves away to go pickpocket some wallets in the city center. And when we made our way to the capital, which was the ends of the earth to us, these members of the hip-hop movement had already flown off to New York.

They would certainly have had little interest in our provincial considerations, but these considerations were what fed our thoughts, and they naturally became the primary material for our first texts. The frustration caused by geographical remoteness pushed us to learn hip-hop culture even better than those creating it in Paris, and we worked very hard at it. The observations caused by the ravages of drugs around us did the rest, and rap was a catharsis for us as well as the means to transmit a message.

> *On était possédé par l'esprit animal "gun blah"*
> *Les milliers d'desperados qui habitent les blocs comme*
>   *moi savent*
> *La vie qu'on avait sombre, grise, quotidien pourri*
> *HLM, immigrés, pauvres ont rêvé tous d'une autre vie*
> *On a pris le rap comme ça, pour s'évader d'la prison*
>   *d'l'existence. . . .**

Translation:

> The animal spirit "gun blah" possessed us
> Thousands of desperados like me living in these
>   concrete towers knew
> The life we had was dark, gray, and just plain rotten

---

*NAP, *"Au sommet de Paris"* ["At the Top of Paris"], from the album *La fin du monde* [The End of the World], Editions Chrysalis Music, France.

Project dwellers, immigrants, the poor all have
dreamed of a better life
This is how we took rap, to escape life's prison.

But this was still not enough for us because we believed that rap
was much more than a new musical genre, and the attraction to Islam
felt by many American rappers made sense to us. Rap led to a spiritual
expression to which we wished to testify without any desire to pros-
elytize whatsoever. Jonathan Franzen* in his book *Pourquoi s'en faire*
says that rappers are the Baudelaire of modern times. In all modesty,
my ambition was to be rap's Seneca or Alain. Rather than reveling
in the evocation of spleen or artificial paradises like so many other
rappers, we decided to speak of faith and education, to show proof of
intelligence and moderation while describing the world of the street.
Today, the majority of those who denigrate rap do not have any idea
what this world is like and do not know what it can bring to young
people like me. All the experiences I had gone through took on meaning because I could now free myself of them by rapping about them.
Islam helped me to transcend them and to warn others who might
be tempted to follow the same path down the slippery slope of easy
money. For me, American rappers were positive role models, a hundred leagues from the "gangsta rap" being served us today, which you
show me as evidence.

Before picking up the threads of my story, I would like to make
a special dedication to Lionel D., Dee Nasty, New Generation MCs,
Saliha, The Littles, Destiné, the whole MA Posse, EJM, Timide et Sans
Complexe, Lucien, Solo, Squat, Maître Madj, Assassin, Mode 2, NTM,
IAM, Ministère Amer, MC Solaar, all the DJs, breakers, and graffiti artists, without forgetting to mention Radio Nova, Rapline, and all those
who took part in the spread of this music in peace, love, and unity. And
not to forget the Americans, especially the Americans, because what-

---

*[Franzen is the white American author of *The Corrections,* which won the Booker Prize
in 2001. —*Trans.*]

ever they can be criticized for, it was they who maintained the sacred fire of hip-hop and Zulu Nation.

When the notoriety of our group went beyond the boundaries of the quarter, my demons came back to the surface. I had an imperious need for money. I could not manage to live a penniless lifestyle. For too long, I had been accustomed to regarding all financial obstacles as minor problems that a little "work" in the city center would be enough to sort out. I could not resign myself to feeling handicapped by my money problems.

At this same time, people began recognizing us in the street in Strasbourg and asked us for our autographs. This was gratifying, but my pockets remained perilously empty. Love of art and the need to tell my story had possessed my body and soul to such an extent that I no longer found the time to refill my pockets. A little voice in my head told me that this situation could not go on indefinitely.

Neuhof had been the zone for quite some time, as boasted by the gleaming BMWs, Mercedes, and Audis of the dealers. Only the "zombiefied" drug addicts that haunted the back streets and parks seemed to be unaware of this reality, preoccupied as they were with discarding their bloodstained syringes in the cellars. Writing our raps from the heart of the furnace was futile; the economic return on our activity was practically nil despite the fact that we were getting paid for our first concerts.

Having realized over time that it had become easier to procure a dose of cocaine or heroin than to pick up a gram of grass, I resolved to adapt to market conditions and start selling shit. I decided to take Majid on as an associate, and I enticed him with the smoothest argument I could dream up: dealing shit would have a regulating effect in the projects by preventing everyone there from falling into hard drugs. In sum, by incarnating as antidealers, we would bring life rather than death.

His hunger for profit eventually overrode his keen sense of morality, and we dug up a supplier in Hautpierre. This latter had begun his career selling stolen cars before diversifying into the resale of valuable items and the sale of hashish at semiwholesale prices. Although still a high school student and a juvenile, he was at the head of a true little mafia. I remember the profound discussions we enjoyed, about life and society; he dreamed of setting up a small garage with honest money while maintaining a cold vision of the world and devoting himself to the veritable worship of money.

Being a good dealer meant being one link in a solid chain. Majid and I reinvested all of our concert money into this activity, and once the quality of the product had been certified, all the elements were in place for building a faithful clientele. The summary marketing survey we took confirmed that our own quarter was the ideal place to set up shop. Methodically, we were guaranteed a quasimonopoly because, except for the rare dealers in ecstasy, nobody offered anything but powder. The shortcoming of this monopoly was that it made us overexposed. We therefore recruited a fourth bandit, a buffoon to whom we would direct our customers to carry out the transactions, while we would be content raking in the money and paying our straw man a commission.

Everyone found what he needed in this arrangement, and our business worked wonderfully. I had succeeded in convincing myself that there was nothing wrong in all of this, and I began moving briskly forward again. Majid was my lieutenant and my right-arm man. We were envied and admired throughout the projects, but very few people knew the source of our revenue; only the other members of the group were abreast of it, and they closed their eyes to our activity. In fact, we never spoke of it, not even in veiled words.

"There are some Gypsies who are looking everywhere for you. . . ." Majid, who no longer lived in the building facing mine but who frequently visited me, turned up on my doorstep in a hurry, flinging this threat at me in a tone that excluded all possibility of a poor joke. He closed the door to my bedroom and sat on Bilal's empty bed. I was still half asleep in my own bed, although the sun was now at its zenith. Sluggishly I mumbled to him: "What's this story you're telling me?"

Several weeks earlier, our understudy had left Strasbourg for good, following his bureaucrat parents, who had been transferred to who knows where. We had had to entrust him with one final mission: liquidate all our merchandise at top speed, which was of poor quality as our wholesaler had burned us for the first time. I knew that sooner or later someone would have to pay for this excessive trust, but I left it up to our loyal and naïve understudy—and quite imprudently, as it turned out, because he was about to leave.

When Majid explained the danger hanging over me, I recalled having actually exchanged several words with a Gypsy before directing him to our guy. For me, even if the Gypsy was from the Polygone neighborhood, he was not dangerous, as he had come to my street all by himself. Furthermore, I had never seen him before, and as he was asking for a fairly substantial quantity of shit, we were not going to let such a windfall slip through our fingers, one that would allow us to quickly rid ourselves of our bad "goods." When, like the cherry on the cake, our understudy reported to me that the customer had not even verified the quality before paying cash, I was convinced that we were dealing with a clown whom we would never hear from again. Apparently, I had been mistaken.

I began to get truly scared. "I didn't sell anything to that guy. I hardly talked with him. He should go complain to our pigeon!" Majid got up and began pacing back and forth across my tiny bedroom.

"We have to do something, we have to do something. . . ." he kept repeating. I, meanwhile, could not see any way out of this mess. But this was the usual routine of our concrete jungle, and I was no coward. Majid knew that I was going to confront the problem one way or another. He only hoped that I would not act rashly in so doing. We had once gotten into a mix-up with two Turks who were much tougher than we were. I had succeeded then, without losing face, by using diplomacy to avoid our getting the beating of our lives. The smile that Majid subsequently bestowed on me, one stretching from ear to ear, was worth any number of thanks.

But in the present situation, the Gypsy had apparently already called in the cavalry. And we were fully aware that once a conflict grew past the one-on-one stage, it became all the harder to manage. In the projects, no one could decently allow themselves to be cheated without complaining, and the Gypsies considered being swindled by a black or an Arab to be the supreme dishonor. Majid knew all this as well as me, and he also knew that the Gypsies would eventually find their way to him after finishing with me. Both of us had in our minds countless examples of poor guys from the neighborhood who had defied the Gypsies by themselves and been found almost dead later. Things had to be calmed down, whatever the cost.

Before doing anything else, I had to conduct my own little investigation. But my efforts to interrogate the guys hanging at the crossroads were fruitless; no one could or wanted to give me any tips. In the street, the family to whom an individual belonged defined how dangerous he was, particularly among the Gypsies. On this scale of values, I was totally insignificant. I had not been a member of any gang for a long time, and my family had absolutely no rank. Who did I take myself for, messing with a Gypsy?

But it was too late for regret. I decided to go see Fat Rachid, who still had a quick mind despite all the junk that he marinated it in. He was always abreast of everything that was done and said in the projects. I found him at the foot of his building talking with three guys I barely knew. Hardly had I shook his hand when explosions started echoing and a gray Golf roared away at top speed. All of us were thrown to the ground, and although no one was hurt, the steel door behind us was dented from the impact of bullets. I had almost crapped my pants. I was now sure that someone was trying to eliminate me, and I found these reprisals completely out of proportion. (I would later learn that this fusillade had strictly nothing to do with me.) Without further ado, I took to my heels. Since our arrival in Neuhof, I had played the bandit, but I had never been in a situation as serious as this one. I was not even known to the police department! For the first time, I lost all the self-assurance I customarily displayed in any and all circumstances.

I was still running when I heard the noise of a van rapidly approaching. It came to a stop when it reached me. I stopped short without daring to look around while my heart beat as if it was about to explode. I closed my eyes.

"Hey, Mademoiselle Schaeffer's teacher's pet!"

I would have recognized that voice out of a hundred! My buddy Mariano! We had gone to primary school together. Not only was Mariano a Gypsy, but his father also was feared and respected in the Polygone neighborhood, and he himself was naturally starting to take over the reins. Still a kid, he played the tough guy but that had not prevented us from sharing a sincere friendship for as long as I can remember. I had lost track of him when I started studying at Saint Anne's, but through rumors I knew that he had become a real big shot in the Polygone and everyone respected him.

He got out of his van and gave me a big smile and a hug before telling me that he had come to Strasbourg to visit his mother because he would be living in the south of France from then on. He explained to me that shortly after his return to the Polygone, he had been told about a black dealer in Neuhof that they were going "to ship back to Africa" because he had ripped off a friend. They were all aware of our system with the straw man and knew that the truly guilty party was the "Negro." Mariano swore that he had instinctively known it was me. He had taken steps to calm the rage of his fellow Gypsies and told me that he had been lurking in the projects for almost an hour to tell me the news in person.

For all Africans, the family structure remains infinitely extendable. I'd experienced this personally, initially through the everyday crowdedness of our apartment, which had regularly been transformed into the HQ of Strasbourg Africanness then over the long haul with families that would eventually become fully grafted to our own. One of these families was the Saboukoulou family. They were Congo natives also, and lived in Hautepierre. The father taught classical literature in middle and high school, and the mother kept house. They had four children, the eldest of whom, Hubert, was from his father's first marriage.

I liked them very much and spent many weekends with them. However, Hubert's parents were going through a divorce. As was standard practice with Congolese families, divorce was finalized after several weeks, and Hubert and his father moved to Neuhof. Quite quickly, Hubert became so close with us that he was considered our real oldest brother, and my mother ended up treating him like one of her own sons. Every day he had lunch or dinner at our apartment.

Hubert was the ideal big brother of the projects: a heavily muscled giant over six feet tall whose presence alone was reassuring. He was always in a good mood and was perpetually smiling, even when sometimes chewing on his lower lip. He spoke impeccable French slowly, and always added at least one word in verlan to every sentence just to make fun of us. He knew the guys in the projects, was abreast of their vices, and avoided them all the more carefully. He never got mixed up in any shady business and, knowing my way of living, avoided judging me with even a look, preferring to preach by example.

Hubert was really one of the good guys; he attended cooking school and dreamed of becoming a chef. I can still remember the unforgettable feast he served us on the eve of his departure for Brazzaville, where he regularly returned to visit his mother. One of my aunts told me how, at the moment of his return to France, he had dressed up in a magnificently embroidered white boubou and insisted on saying good-bye to everyone in the family, without exception.

Hubert never returned. He died in September 1989 above the Ténéré Desert in the explosion of the UTA DC10 that was taking him back to France. He was twenty-one years old. He should have missed his flight because of a reservation error or something of that nature. It is true, "We are Gods and to God we return."* I mourned Hubert

---

*Qur'an 2:156.

that entire year. I remained convinced, however, that there had been a mistake, that he had backed out at the last moment and ultimately had not caught this flight. The fact that his clothes had been found was no doubt due to the fact that his baggage had made the journey without the passenger, as sometimes happens. He would reappear and tell us something in verlan before bursting out laughing. But . . . he never came back.

Therefore, life went on, with my studies and rap, and my impassioned reading, but also with my increasing interrogations on money, drugs, and death. During the Toussaint vacation [November 1, All Saint's Day] that I spent in Paris with Bilal, an event occurred that proved to be a major turning point for me on this journey that still had not found any direction.

During our visits to Paris, I was in the habit of spending entire days and evenings in discussion with my cousin Frédéric. I had the feeling of maintaining with him a relationship of mutual and free exchange, to which I gave myself wholeheartedly and with no ulterior motives, as if I were emptying a piece of myself with each of our conversations. Until that point, I had strictly conformed to the basic life guidelines of the projects, operating only on the basis of what was profitable for me, despite the doubts that still remained in the domain of what went unsaid. None of the relations I could weave with another were neutral; I weighed the egotistical self-advantage that this action or that word could bring me. Beneath my cultural veneer, I remained a boy of the streets, a little crook whose only thought was to protect himself and to impose his will. My intelligence coldly executed the commands that my arrogance provided. But all of this finally crumbled away with the death of Hubert, which allowed me to experience limitation for the first time. I discovered I was still a child and I was scared.

That day I was strolling through the streets of Plessis-Robinson where my "Parisian family" lived, and I explained my theory about the misfortune of the projects to Frédéric. Le Plessis was not in the zone, and it formed a physical and emotional respite for me, and for the first time, I was openly examining myself, my destiny, and the destiny of my fellows. You have to consider what the projects really are, was what I was basically explaining to my cousin. You must understand and make understandable the desolation and inner poverty of those who live there. I am not saying it's impossible for them to experience moments of happiness, but all of them are suffering because they did not choose the situation they are in and it seems to them that they are stuck in it forever. The tragedy of the projects is the determinism that rules people's lives and their awareness of an inescapable fate from which their misfortune originates. The reckless quest for money whereby everything is permitted stems from this; money certainly does not bring happiness, but it does offer people choices.

This is how we naturally began speaking about religion. The actual content of our conversation was of little importance, and if I could listen to it again today, I would surely smile at the naïveté of our pseudo-metaphysical arguments. But for me it was not the kind of discussion you would hear in the Café du Commerce. I poured all of my anxieties and questions of the moment into it.

My faith was real. Off-beat, certainly, but real. After all, God was omnipresent in my life: in the attitude and words of my mother, in the vision of the world offered me at Saint Anne's, in the exalted remarks that Bilal made to me following his conversion. The existence of God was my sole certainty, but the idea of religion was one I found difficult to grasp. Of course, I went to Mass sometimes on Sunday, I had been baptized and taken my first communion, I had sung in different choruses. As a choirboy, I had been chosen to read the texts during certain services, and more than once I had meditated alone in the chapel.

But it was not long before I began having questions about the Catholic doctrine, and these questions prevented me from accepting it completely. How could I understand the Trinity and the divinity of Christ, and how could it manifest in my life and in my everyday thoughts? I tried to find my answer while ceaselessly questioning those around me. I had carefully listened to the counsel of Monsieur Leborgne, Sister François, and later on, Monsieur Miry, during catechism and religious education classes, but they did not cast much light on this question for me—which was more personal and existential than theological. Unable to find Christ in my heart, I began looking for him with the tools of reason, but I still did not understand, and I did not understand *myself.*

I finally collided headlong into a problem that caused me to vacillate: why did God, who created us, make it so difficult to understand Him?

This impassioned conversation, in which I shared with Frédéric all my questions, finished with this insoluble contradiction. But it unleashed a general requestioning of my entire life and all the values on which I had constructed myself—or believed that I had. On my return to Strasbourg after my Parisian vacation, I had the impression of being a grenade from which the pin had been pulled. Bilal, to whom I had confided my doubts on the train home, recommended several books that I devoured feverishly over the next several nights. Now, for the first time, the answers they offered resonated inside of me.

Now everything was very clear. This Muslim religion I had long brushed alongside through the person of my brother, and toward which I turned today, suddenly took on for me the strength of evidence. Islam was my natural religion, the one that Abraham, the "first believer" (*hanif*), had witnessed initially. I glued the pieces back together, happy as I had never been before.

"I swear there is no other God but Allah and Muhammad is his prophet!"

I clearly and slowly articulated the *shahada*—the swearing of Muslim faith in Arabic—with my index finger pointed toward the sky and my body still dripping from the copious ablutions. This was an important day, and I felt it. It was, as well, an important day for Majid; he had pronounced the shahada right before me and was listening to me repeat it, with a big smile on his face.

Fifteen days after my return from Paris, I had called him simply to ask: "What if we went to the mosque?" Majid was a native of Algeria, from a Berber family of Kabylia, and had been born in Cherchell, a little town near Algiers. Although Muslim, his parents had drifted from their Islamic education once in France, keeping only the fast of Ramadan and retaining a little folklore. So Majid at the start knew as much as I did about Islam, which is to say not much. When arranging our rendez-vous, we had exchanged a knowing look because we were fully aware of the implications of committing ourselves to this path, implications that leapt immediately to our minds.

"Okay for the mosque," he answered me, "but you know that we cannot continue to be dealers . . . and we, in fact, will have to get rid of everything connected to it!" I agreed with him.

We therefore chucked out the remaining "product" and burned a ton of new clothes bought with "criminal money." Still, for the fateful day, we chose the mosque in the center of the city rather than the one in the projects, as we were not too keen to undergo the disapproving gaze of the old hadj who had known us when we were sowing our wild oats. The grand mosque of Strasbourg was separated from the Lycée Notre Dame des Mineurs, which I was now attending, only by a simple wall. However, and I don't know why, we looked for the entrance all afternoon and even had to ask directions from an orthodox Jew dressed in traditional fashion. He opened his eyes wide on hearing our request and favored us with a discreet smile before going on his way. He must have thought we were playing a joke on him, which obviously was not the case.

Several months passed since this first day, during which we had learned the five pillars of Islam—the swearing of faith, prayer, fasting during the month of Ramadan, purifying social tax, and pilgrimage to Mecca—as well as the methods of Islam—how to make one's ablutions, how to recite the *fatiha* (the first verses of the Qur'an) in Arabic and the three final *suras* (chapters), how to perform the fast, and so forth. We were already familiar with the grand mosque on the day we officially became Muslims. By this act, we joined our fates with those of an entire community, symbolized by the two brothers who witnessed our adhesion to Islam.

I became Abd al Malik. My life was henceforth governed by the rhythm of the five daily prayers, and I no longer ate pork or any meat that had not been sacrificed in accordance with the *halal* rite. My mother took my conversion as proof of good morality, and soon, by dint of conversations, the sentiments of my family evolved from indifference to curiosity, and finally culminated in a true interest in Islamic thought. Our parents and relatives—my mother in Strasbourg and my aunt in Plessis—showed evidence of sincere open-mindedness by accepting the fact that their children, one after the other, embraced a faith that was not their own.

My mother even told me that religion was only a means, that only the end counted. This woman, who had known only Catholicism her entire life, accepted, without any disproportionate emotion, the fact that her sons would not continue a family spiritual tradition dating from before her grandparents. I only became aware of the grandeur of her attitude much later; at that time, nothing had the power to surprise me insofar as "truth cannot help but triumph over error!"

I thereby made the transition from a state of radical doubt to one of complete observance. My criminal reflexes dissolved in this new nature, although no signs of this appeared on the surface, as my misdeeds had always been discreet. I became someone else entirely, at the cost of a definitive rupture with a part of who I was. From this time forward, I ceaselessly worked on strengthening my faith, spending the bulk of my time reading and educating myself. At the *lycée,* I would pester my teachers who taught human science to recommend reference books for me. I read everywhere—at home, in mass transit, and during breaks at school—and this passion for reading has never left me. I fed on all kinds of learning, sacred and profane, but I was especially interested in anything that pursued the same direction I was taking, everything and anything that could help magnify Islam, everything and anything that could demonstrate to me the superiority of the Muslim religion over all the other traditions of religious, philosophical, and moral thought.

This attentiveness and fervor were not foreign to my success in school. Soon, with my *bac** for literature in my pocket, full of confidence with my seventeen out of twenty in philosophy—the highest grade in the Lower Rhine region—I enrolled in the School of Classic Literature of the University of Human Sciences in Strasbourg.

For my mother, it was as if I had walked on the moon.

---

*[*Bac* is short for *baccalauréat,* roughly the French equivalent of a high school diploma. —*Trans.*]

THREE

ISLAM OF THE BANLIEUE

My friends laugh at me, and I'm ashamed to talk of my
  difference
If they leave me the absence will transform into an even
  greater suffering than the one emptying me
What do I have or else what don't I have?!
Who am I or else who am I not?!
Every day I bury myself a little deeper in this hole that
  thinks it's me
Even this melancholy people call cool hurts me
I could almost say how many stars there are in the sky
In spiritual terms there are too many mysteries in the
  quest into myself

FROM THE SONG "TRACES OF LIGHT"

As-salat khayru min an-nawm. . . . [Prayer is better than sleep. . . .] I
was usually the first to wake in the apartment. Immediately after my
ablutions, I would slip into my white *djellaba,* a symbol of modesty and
purity, cover my head with a woolen *chéchia,* and open a small, transpar-
ent vial to sprinkle myself with perfumed oil. With cautious steps so as
to not awaken anybody as it was still night, I would make my way to

the small three-room apartment that served as a mosque on the ground floor of the facing building.

A hadj, with authority conferred upon his words by having accomplished the pilgrimage to Mecca, had explained to us one day after prayer that the way we dressed and the image we had of ourselves greatly influenced our inner life. I had, in fact, noted that myself. Every Friday, when I decided to dress in strict *sunna* fashion, which is to say traditionally, I felt a state of specific "devotional concentration" develop inside of me—and it made me proud. Whenever I visited a mosque other than the one in the projects and I was dressed this way, non-Muslims stared at me while I made my way there, and at this I felt a certain joy. I had a feeling of being part of a community that had not been imposed upon me but which I had become a member of by my own free will. This demarcation, which set me off from the masses, gave me the sensation of living fully and of having finally found my own identity, signified by the white sunna garb that I soon started wearing every morning.

The imam was the first to arrive at the mosque. Always impeccable, he was a man of average size, in his thirties, with a salt-and-pepper beard. The dark circles under his eyes gave him an air of serenity and power. He was a native of the city of Fez in Morocco, and although he spoke French in a halting fashion, he understood it quite well. The fact that he was foreign and did not always grasp how the youth of the projects reasoned did not bother me at all. Later, I would harbor doubts about his ability to guide us through this world that was even stranger to him than it was to us. But for the time being, the touch of the exotic that he offered gave me a glimpse of the universality and diversity that gives Islam its character. After opening the door of the mosque-apartment, he would settle back in his office, whose door he left ajar while he read the Qur'an or other traditional texts. Most of the time, I was the third one to remove my shoes, tread the Oriental rugs, and make the two *rakaat* (ritual prostrations) that are de rigueur upon entering a mosque. In addition to the imam, the old hadj Biyoud was generally already there. Every morning he followed a never-changing ritual: he opened the windows, drew the curtains, and aired out the rooms, always in the same order. I would then sit down near the radiator beneath the window looking out over rue de Périgueux and read the Qur'an while waiting for the *adhen,* the call to prayer. The small mosque was far from being filled when, after performing the two rakaat, the imam pronounced the *takbir: Allah ou akbar,* "God is the greatest." Then he opened with the prayer of the *subh* (the obligatory morning prayer). The three of us remained in total concentration until the final *"Salaam oua likoum,"* "May peace be upon you." And peace *was* upon us: seated with our hands resting on our knees, our heads turned from right to left, when each of us returned home, the light was upon our lips.

I appreciated these moments when the first light of morning began to emerge and was welcomed joyously by the songs of invisible birds and one could taste a light breeze caressing one's face. When I got back home, everyone was still asleep. In my room, I took off my chéchia, then my djellaba, and plunged back into my still lukewarm bed.

After eating breakfast with my family, I headed off to class for the day. At the end of the afternoon, immediately upon my return to the projects, I tried to memorize the prayers I had forgotten. After I did my homework and a little reading, and after eating dinner, I would go meet my brothers at the mosque. Majid had told me how, when Machiavelli had been removed from power, he sought refuge with woodcutters and adopted their manners, language, and clothing. However, once he returned home, he reassumed his true identity by donning the ceremonial dress of the Florentine dignitary he had concealed in his suitcase. I was never able to verify this anecdote, but it affected me so deeply that when I left the context of the outside society—school, administration, and so on—I slipped on a djellaba or a Pakistani outfit (*shalwar-kamiz*) that I wore, of course, with a variety of chéchias. Because I was now letting myself grow a beard, I therefore conformed in every aspect to the idea of my true nature that I was creating for myself. Régis, the former me, died and was reborn as Abd al Malik. Dressed this way, I was both one and a multitude, an individual and a community of close to a billion people spread throughout the world. I felt strong.

In the evening at the mosque, between the prayers of the *maghrib* (sunset) and the *isha* (final prayer), we read a collection of *hadiths,* the traditional tales of the Prophet Muhammad (PSL*) that transmit, outside of the Qur'an, his gestures and words of wisdom. Five or six of us would also gather together every Saturday evening to study and then stay up together. These vigils were punctuated with classes in Islamic jurisprudence, studies of the life of the Prophet Muhammad (PSL) and others in Islam in general. We read the Qur'an and the hadiths together until dawn, the whole divided by prayers and religious discussions. These *mudakara* (traditional debates) consisted of placing oneself in a hypothetical situation and then determining the correct "Islamic attitude" to adopt in such a scenario.

I recall being tortured by such "fundamental" questions as to whether or not it was licit to shake the hand of a woman when greeting her, or whether or not watching a film at the cinema or on television was compatible with "the ban on representation." I was so permeated by this atmosphere in which the distinction between licit and illicit (*halal* and *haram*) became an obsession that even today, I have to confess, I am sometimes caught by this kind of legalistic question quite by chance. Whenever I am introduced to a person of the opposite sex, I believe it is my habit to behave in a polite and welcoming way—in a word, naturally! And yet, from time to time, I am disconcerted to note the involuntary return of the question: Should I or should I not shake her hand? And then to my great displeasure, I have a brief hesitation!

It should be said that the female gender and the appropriate relations to have with them were often our major concern. They embodied a form of temptation to be avoided at all cost. Given this point of view, a number of brothers who contemplated marriage were fraught with guilt. It was from this perspective that I considered the question of the

---

*[*Paix et Salut sur Lui* (Peace and Salvation upon Him). —*Trans.*]

hijab (Islamic veil) during this period. It was just simply a sure means of never being subjected to temptation.

I often happened to unearth in the imam's library a booklet dedicated to the great saint and poet Rabya al'Adawiya, who lived in eighth-century Iraq and who had formed a federation of numerous male disciples. This had momentarily shaken my convictions, but my vision of the world remained quite limited and regulated, truly binary, and, in the final analysis, barely internalized. I lived Islam as a body of commandments that I only needed to scrupulously put into practice. My satisfaction was made all the greater by noting everything that my discipline was allowing me to escape. While we were keeping vigil, the youth at the foot of the buildings were smoking joints and knocking back one can after another of 8.6—those well-known half-liter cans of Dutch beer that are 8.6 proof. They would drink and carry on, shouting unbelievable insanities and violently fighting among themselves when everything else had worn them out.

Most of the time the whole scene was enlivened by the squealing tires of stolen cars—a kind of background music. We, on the other hand, were certainly not large in number, but our meetings took place in an atmosphere that was serious and one of real solidarity. Of course, Majid and I were already close, but the others had become our brothers in Islam, and this held great value in our eyes. Some of them who had mastered the Arabic language let us profit from their knowledge, whether it was regarding the correct pronunciation of verses from the Qur'an or having to do with learning the orthographic and grammatical basics of the language.

At that time, our ideal was to live as Muslims had during the time of the Prophet (PSL) as it was described to us in the books of piety. For us, the modern Western world, with its insipid and materialistic values, its contempt of dignity and human spirituality, constituted an aberration in history, a cancer even, that only Islam had the tools to cure. And of course, as Muslims immersed in this Western reality, we were in a particularly good position to criticize and correct this state of affairs.

This black-and-white vision made it so that at any moment, despite the apparent candor of our utopian considerations, there was a risk that feelings of hatred could rise back to the surface. Even if we did not harbor any violent intentions, by virtue of debasing the modern context in which we lived, the worst kinds of verbal excesses flourished beneath a discourse that was a priori quite moralistic. All the more so as this rejection of our surroundings could easily be shored up by a very concrete reality, which we had rapidly worked on interpreting by assuming roles as its victims.

Hadn't we all suffered humiliations during simple but systematic identity checks? Hadn't some of us been victims of police violence? How many of our peers had we lost to car chases in which they had been pursued by the BAC*? How many "police blunders" or the strong suspicion of a desire to kill a "nigger" or a "wog" had never led to any convictions? Who among us had not been mortified by the vexations and patent racism inherent in our dealings with the police, our work colleagues, and/or government officials? Not to mention the fact that all of us, for two generations, had been in difficult social and/or family situations. Finally, any event that affected us even a little was capable of toppling our Islamic altruism into total, unrestrained hatred of the West.

We also fed our fervor with the videocassettes and short books of Ahmed Deedat, a self-taught South African Muslim preacher of Indian origin who had become a polemicist. His enflamed diatribes against the highest authorities of Christianity confirmed our point of view about the cultural, moral, and even religious decadence of Western civilization. The critical distance that I attempted to maintain toward this discourse still allowed me to realize that these books and videos, which we obtained from an Islamic bookstore near the Strasbourg train station, encouraged us to swell with a disproportionate sense of pride.

While the sly rhetoric of this preaching did not contain any overt

---

*[The *Brigade Anti-Criminalité* is a branch of the police that is specially trained to deal with violence in the *banlieues* (projects). —*Trans.*]

appeal for us to become inflamed with hatred, its effect was well contrived: buried in his ignorance and blinded by his own lies, the other—the Christian, the Westerner—deserved only our condescending commiseration and, in the end, counted for nothing. This lack of respect sometimes made me ill at ease. However, I was far from realizing that I truly did not know Islam in depth, that what I *did* know of it was only what some people had wished to tell me about it, and that its message did not have much in common with their mediocre discourses. Drowning in this spiritual fog, I remained convinced—despite the reservations that I clearly continued to harbor and took pains to conceal during our meetings—that I was on the road to truth, that we were saved, and that all others were racing to their own ruin if they did not follow us.

Our average age was a problem for me. The mosque was only frequented by older men, elderly men, in fact. I found this unacceptable. The youth were right there, however, they were in the streets all around the mosque! We did everything we could to attract them, because, after all, even if they were muggers, dealers, thieves, or even doped up, hadn't they all, for the most part, been born Muslim? And if it was so hard to appropriate another culture, wouldn't the obvious step be to draw nearer to oneself? What is closer to one's self than God, "who is closer to you than your jugular vein"?

The light was there, I told myself, if we could only help them to open their eyes . . . . But when I aired these proselytizing impulses in our Saturday evening meetings, even if all the brothers showed their approval of what I said, no one suggested any concrete actions. Having nothing in my own head in this regard either, I remained completely frustrated, and this eventually began obsessing me so much that it caused me to lose sleep.

Then one day, during the month of Ramadan 1994, following the afternoon prayer, while I was preparing to return home, I was stopped short by an impromptu speech: "*Salaam oua likoum. . . ,*" "I ask your attention, if you please, dear brothers. . . ." Three young bearded men with turbans and dressed in Pakistani style had stood up before this gathering of the faithful, at the side of an imam who remained seated cross-legged, reciting the traditional invocations in silence. One of these three young men, the most physically imposing one, continued: "Praise to God who has permitted us to perform the prayer of *'asr,* which the Prophet Muhammad (PSL) said was one of the most important prayers, together with that of the subh. But what does this have to do with your sons, our brothers, your daughters, our sisters, who are hanging out in the streets with nothing better to do than to destroy themselves?"

I sat back down in a daze. These three brothers, whom I had never seen before, were spelling out what I had dreamed of hearing for months! I was crazed with joy.

The brother continued his speech by saying that it was incumbent upon every Muslim to spread Islam because "the Muslim loves for his brother what he loves for himself." Because Islam was the solution to all our misfortunes, I drank in every one of his words. I was so impressed by the erudition, self-confidence, and charisma of this young orator that, at the end of his speech, when he asked who was ready to follow him on the *fi sabillah,* "on the path of God" or "for the cause of God," I raised my hand without even being aware that I was doing so. I saw another arm also being raised without hesitation at the other end of the room. It was Majid. We were the only two to take this step that afternoon. After the mosque had emptied, Majid and the three brothers and I all sat down together in a circle.

I had never before seen people who acted like these three individuals. When they spoke to us they always looked us straight in the eye, and they expressed themselves gently but firmly, in a way that was both clear and audible. Their sentences never died away unfinished. They punctuated each of their sentences with a *mash'Allah!,* "if it please God," an expression used to denote admiring approval, or else an *'ajib!,* "extraordinary" or "wonderful." They never missed an opportunity to call down God's blessing upon us with incessant *barka 'allahu fik!,* "may God's blessing be upon you."

They told us that they lived in Schiltigheim and Koenigshoffen. Formerly, one had been a drug addict, one a thief, and one a pimp. Without Islam, they said, they would have ended up in prison or in an asylum, if not the morgue. They owed a debt to God, they declared, and helping other youth who were enslaved as they had been was, for them and for Islam, both a responsibility and an act of grace. They next told us that they were members of the Tablighi Brotherhood, Islamic preachers who have "departed upon the path of God." According to them, this movement had been born in India in 1927 and was inspired by the preaching of a certain Muhammed Ilyas, a man who had assumed the mission of revitalizing Islam by inciting Muslims to model their behavior on the exemplary life of the Prophet (PSL).

Of these three brothers, the most loquacious was the one who had delivered the impromptu speech before the assembly. After several seconds, he told us more explicitly: "When one departs upon God's path, one attempts to acquire several *sifat* (qualities) displayed by the companions of the Prophet (PSL). These qualities are the following: First, the good news—'No other God before Allah, Muhammad is his Prophet.' Second, praying with concentration and devotion. Third, religious science and the remembrance of God's name (*dhikr*). Fourth, generosity toward fellow Muslims. Fifth, sincerity of intention. And finally the sixth, to preach the religion of Allah and 'to depart upon his path.'" He finished the enumeration of this list by quoting a hadith: "Among the qualities of a good Muslim is that of not getting mixed up in matters that do not concern him!" I was fascinated by these words; they seemed to me to be simultaneously vigorous, structured, and intentional—and even today I can recall them exactly as I was led to repeat them a countless number of times.

The three brothers finally explained to us what the fact of "departing on the road of God" concretely consisted of by explaining how several different programs of varying duration were possible: one of three days—in fact, a weekend from Friday evening to Sunday afternoon—one of ten days, one of forty days, one of four months, and finally one that lasted an entire year. "But," said the large, bearded fellow with a laugh, "you can begin with the one of three days!"

Returning home I was unable to stop thinking about this encounter. I spoke to Bilal about it the next day and wasted no time overcoming his initial reservations and convincing him of our duty to "depart." I had soon successfully persuaded the other members of NAP of the imperious legitimacy of the movement of Muhammed Ilyas and the necessity to become part of it. I also enrolled the brothers who participated in our Saturday evening meetings. Majid only informed me later that they had been, in fact, familiar with this movement far longer than we were. When seeing my enthusiasm, they had not dared admit this to me personally, fearing that I would reproach them for not having suggested the *tabligh* as a solution to that frustration that had been eating away at me for months.

Barely one week after our encounter with the three preachers, we had already formed a *jama'at,* a group of a dozen or so persons who were more than motivated and ready to opt early on for the "weekend program." The eve of the following weekend, we all made our way to the Mosque of Koenigshoffen, from which, generally speaking, all the groups of Strasbourg had spread. It was planned that we would visit Colmar and Saint-Avold, where other brothers of the tabligh, forewarned of our arrival, would welcome us to their mosque.

Of the three preachers whom we had met in Neuhof, only two, the less loquacious ones, would accompany us—the large, bearded fellow had "departed" for four months in Spain. I was not especially surprised by the efficiency and internationalism of the movement. They, conversely, were quite impressed, they told me, by the speed with which I had pulled together a group. They were not stingy with praise for my efforts, and in what was a supreme honor, they asked for divine blessing upon me and my entire family, after I had supplied the fifty francs to cover various expenses.

The crew was then divided into two groups of seven persons each, and after discussion, the two brothers were designated as the heads (emirs) of each of them. I was part of the group that made its way to Saint-Avold in a blue minivan. We drove there on the Nationale,* which cut through countless villages. During the trip, our emir had us recite, in turn, the last ten suras of the Qur'an after he had personally made the invocation specific to travel so that our sojourn would be blessed. He then insisted that we guard our silence and only repeat, in low voices while saying our rosary, the first part of the shahada: *La ilaha illa'llah,* "There is no God but Allah." Simultaneous with our doing this, he told us a story that I would be led to relate, in turn, on numerous occasions.

Here is the basic plot:

In France, two brothers, given the responsibility of escorting a venerable Pakistani sheik who had "departed on the path of God," had forgotten to fill their gas tank and ran the risk of breaking down at any moment in the middle of the country and in the middle of the night. The old man took out his rosary, told the two brothers not to stop, come what may, and began to silently repeat the shahada. They traveled more than three hundred miles with a completely empty tank.

Today, I smile—or grimace—at such gullibility. But during this time, I was so in quest of the marvelous, in a world where nothing could surprise me, that this kind of story was the stuff to make me dream. All of us were more or less in this same position, and these preposterous tales welded the group around the feeling that we were sharing a unique adventure.

In Saint-Avold, we spent three days praying, preaching in the streets, learning—mainly learning verses from the Qur'an by heart—and engaging in discussions in the mosque of our hosts. Our time was divvied

---

*[The Nationale was the main road connecting the cities of France before the thruway was built. —*Trans.*]

up between *da'wa* (sermons) and *khidma* (ordinary tasks), all under the supervision of our emir. Every evening following the last prayer, we joyfully shared a meal and then read tales of the lives of the companions of the Prophet (PSL). Following this, each person would unfold his down sleeping bag, transforming the prayer hall into a dormitory.

One day, Cherif, a young man of Algerian origin from the region of Sochaux (who would later be our emir for a trip to Besançon), told us that we should never be seen either eating or sleeping by the brothers who had welcomed us to their mosque. Instead, we should appear to be almost like angels so that our words would leave an even more profound impression upon them. In the morning after the prayer of sunrise, we drew up the day's agenda before going back to bed until around nine o'clock, at which time we ate a small breakfast. Next, we recited or learned verses from the Qur'an, hadiths, or else the sifat (the essential qualities for companions). Immediately after the noon prayer, before the mosque emptied, we fervently urged the faithful present to join with us. Following the noon meal, those persuaded by our appeal met us again, and we went out together.

We traveled through the streets in groups of four: an emir (a new one would be named if the emir of the entire group was not part of the group), a spokesman, a guide (most often chosen from among our hosts based on his knowledge of the area and its inhabitants), and an "invoker" (who in reality generally remained at the mosque and whose sole duty was to invoke the name of God until the return of his group).

All the "departures on the path of God" invariably took place in this fashion in accordance with an organization that was intended to be meticulous. "Departing" was putting oneself in the same position as the companions of the Prophet (PSL) who spread Islam throughout the world. This memory was one that had to remain constantly in the minds of all those who "departed," and the brothers of the tabligh gave particular emphasis (as did the entire community, incidentally) to this element of intention. Therefore, before going out on the road, the emir took it upon himself to ask each member of his group to individually and collectively renew their intention, thereby ensuring that the project would meet with God's approval.

Caught in this pious if not sanctimonious atmosphere and in the enthusiasm of these actions, I soon dedicated myself to making my way through the whole of France to preach. During my wanderings, I encountered a multitude of extremely colorful figures, each as exalted as the next. I remember one white convert, Yahya, who wore a white turban and a red djellaba, whom I met in Sochaux. He explained to me how only the tabligh movement was capable of profoundly changing the lives of believers, that conferences and abstract speeches served no purpose. He explained how it was necessary to live like the companions of the Prophet (PSL) in everyday life, continuing, of course, to preach in the streets, and how this was the way one could understand Islam.

I can also recall the brothers I met in the Parisian suburbs whose entire family was tabligh, and also Majid of Marseille, who had already "departed" several times to India, Pakistan, and Bangladesh. A former hardened criminal who had once been the scourge of the region, he happily told anyone who would listen how he had been diagnosed with HIV, but that following his first four-month "departure on the path of God," he had the divine surprise to hear a diagnosis that the virus had quite simply completely disappeared from his body. One doctor even allegedly said that he had the blood of a newborn!

We went everywhere to preach the message of Islam, everywhere that the youth of North African, black African, and Turkish origin could be found: the project stairwells reeking of urine, darkened cellars, shabby bars, and even the least-engaging of streets, places where one could get their throat slashed. We even went to university campuses. At times we managed to approach whites, but only if they seemed to display an interest or if there was a converted white among our number.

If the "fishing" had been fruitful, our group would attract five or six people, perhaps more, who would return to the mosque with us. There, around a glass of mint tea or some pistachios or peanuts, we would draw up a picture of the grandeur and nobility of Islam for them. Before the afternoon prayer, each individual was then free to go about one's personal business inside the mosque, but the majority opted to take a well-deserved siesta. This was generally the moment chosen by the emir (who had numerous "departures" under his belt), to relay miraculous stories like the one of the "empty gas tank."

During the sunset prayer, the mosques were often full to bursting. The emir would wait for the end of the prayer to give an enthusiastic speech on the believer's responsibility, a discourse skillfully peppered with Qur'anic verses and hadiths.

At the risk of surprising some people and revolting others, I must confess that I do not have a bad memory of these "departures" and the meetings punctuating them. For me they proved to be a veritable school of life, with both positive and negative aspects. By going out to preach in the field, I learned to consider the ignorance and poverty of my peers from a new perspective. The misunderstanding displayed by the young with regard to their own religion was merely the reflection of a certain lack of knowledge about themselves, their roots, and the collective memories of their parents. Social poverty made them, for the most part, partially deaf to a discourse that considered material well-being secondary and negligible when compared to spiritual things. It is true that this essential realization was presented to them in a form that was moralizing, dogmatic, and actually fairly infantile. But this does not lessen the urgency of its necessity. . . .

From these departures, I also realized that the problem of the projects was not merely social; it did not concern the situation of the *group,* but first and foremost the relationship of the *individual to himself*—his responsibility toward himself. I read this not only in the gazes of all the youth I met in my journeys across France, but also in the life I experienced within the very heart of the tabligh structure. The example of khidma service, almost bordering on caricature, clearly illustrates what I discovered during this period.

The brothers in charge had to assume responsibility for organizing the shopping and the meals, and sometimes even found themselves entrusted with the financial management of the group. This was educational and instructive for everybody, especially for the young who, like me, belonged to that generation where easy money flowed in torrents when one knew how to get it and who considered their parents to be buffoons who just could not seem to comprehend the workings of the system. Thanks to this accelerated education in daily realities, each of us was able to grasp the extent of the financial and domestic worries our parents constantly faced.

Furthermore, this hierarchical organization, with the emir at the top, allowed each of us to understand the necessity for authority and respect if the group was to function properly.

Because these ideas had been given legitimacy by Islam, they were more readily and easily accepted, even by those who had been most resistant in their former lives. When someone like me has grown up in a ghetto neighborhood, it is not difficult to realize how the lack of authority there presented a major problem. And parents, who are generally caught in the clutches of extremely precarious living situations, even as loving and well intentioned as most of them are, cannot, in the majority of cases, do anything about this. Placed in a position of obvious social inferiority, they are perceived as weak, and their authority loses its natural legitimacy. It is usurped by those who can and do furnish the young with the means to achieve success—as fragile, illusory, and criminal as this success may be. Almost all young people who, like me, found themselves "departing on the path of God" had been more or less in open conflict with authority. At least our proselytizing expeditions had the virtue of toppling this perverse arrangement.

But they were also responsible for instituting another arrangement, one that was equally perverse. We put all of these salutary challenges to past assumptions to work, with our ultimate goal being the Islamicization of everything surrounding us. I was not the last person to reinforce this system, and I rejected everything that was not heading in its direction—in *my* direction. We alone would hold the truth that could rid the world of the evil rotting it, embodied, in our eyes, by modern Western civilization and its retinue of false values.

After several months, our preaching—supported by the communication tools provided us by the tabligh—had managed to fill the mosque of Neuhof with young converts. For the first time, the category of the elder faithful was in the minority. A majority of the new recruits had converted or returned to Islam after having crossed my path or Majid's. A champion proselytizer, in my projects I had become an Islamic figure. This was all I lived for.

When I was not "departing," I preached at the base of our apartment building, in front of the minimart and the tobacco shop, and even on the street corners—everywhere the young hung out together. Often, when they saw me coming they would throw their joints away or conceal their cans of beer. They would all listen to me describe the greatness of the divine, the tortures of the tomb and of Hell, or the delights of Paradise. I would always spot one person in the crowd who seemed attentive, and I would concentrate my efforts on him until I managed to drag him back to the mosque.

There was a sense of urgency for me about this mission. It was important to save our brothers whatever the cost. I spent every evening either at the neighborhood mosque or at a mosque in another community. Attending teaching circles of other young Muslims who had organized themselves using us as an example filled us with pride and hope. Soon, there was not a single mosque in Strasbourg or the surrounding area that was unknown to me. I had become the informal spokesman of a certain form of Islam in the projects.

It was during this period that Majid and I, certainly because of our exalted speeches, were contacted by brothers who had a vision for spreading Islam that was "explosive" to say the least. This was in 1995, when the Kelkal affair was still at its height in Port Royal. Kelkal was the name of the young man from Lyon who was accused of planting plastic explosive in the rails of the TGV [high-speed rail line] and was suspected of being a member of the terrorist group responsible for the bombing of the RER.* Following an ambush whose aim, apparently, was not to capture Kelkal alive, he ended up on a slab. Most Muslims felt that his life had been disposed of, if not brutally, at least casually, as if it was not worth the trouble of bringing him to justice.

Projects and posh neighborhoods alike were buzzing about nothing except this polemic. So we were hardly surprised when two brothers, who Majid and I knew fairly well, buttonholed us to ask what we thought about the matter. After the de rigueur *salaam* and a few minutes spent making small talk, we spent several minutes on this topic. Then the more taciturn of the pair, whose confidence was at ease in the company of two bearded guys like ourselves, suddenly blurted out: "What if we, too, did something? These *kufar* (heathens) don't like us at all, soon they will be shooting us down like rabbits!"

His alter ego then chimed in: "We are ready to blow up the prefecture, join us. . . ." We initially thought this was a joke. But our two interlocutors made it perfectly clear that they were not playing around. We were stupefied and could hardly believe our ears. But we wasted no time sending them packing, and we did not see them hanging around our neighborhood again.

Certainly we were filled with a total faith, a seamless block of belief that caused us to lose our appreciation of subtlety and often even our critical senses. But all the same we had not become complete idiots! Despite the very rudimentary logic of our discourses, Majid and I were never motivated by hate. We found pleasure in a certain anti-Western ideology, but the thought of making the move from verbal animosity to physical violence never popped into our minds.

We were first and foremost motivated by the positive and utopian aspects of this ideology—which it has—and wanted nothing to do with the angry madmen claiming to be on our side. Furthermore, we were instinctively distrustful of these two fellows and had smelled a provocation in their words. Like the narcs who convince drug addicts to sell out

---

*[The RER is the Reseau Express Regional, specifically, the Regional Express Network, which is the rapid transit system serving Paris and its suburbs. —*Trans.*]

their dealers in order to stay out of prison, we knew that the RG had informers in the mosques paid with promises of naturalization. Later, rumors circulated that indicated that the two lascars in question had been recruited in this way and that they were trying to entrap us, but this was never confirmed.

Time passed. Life flowed more peacefully at home. My brothers were Muslims in their fashion, which is to say they expressed their faith much more simply than I did. Bilal, even if he had been the first among us to convert, had not altered his fundamental lifestyle—never satisfied with anything and complaining about everything, loving to laugh, and "enjoying life to the full," as he liked to say. He began praying more seriously after earning his degree in general mechanics at the Marais Technical School in Schiltigheim and justified his change of heart this way:

> A guy in my class, Nouredine, did not give a damn about any-thing for the entire year, he was a real *hmarr* [ass] and never went to class. One day he showed up, I swear, completely changed. He talked about Islam, he made the *salat* and everything, and got his diploma with his fingers up his nose. Me, I had been humping like a madman for the whole year! I wept, I pleaded, I asked Rabbi [Teacher, i.e., God], and it was only by doing all that, that I was able to get my diploma. Now the reason I pray is that, to give thanks. Just ask Mustapha. . . .

Bilal and Mustapha had been best friends since forever. In the same class at middle school, they were tight as thieves and went to the same technical school. They had been burglars together, were arrested together, went out with the same girls. . . . And since the time of the NAP venture, Karim and Muhammed, who had joined them, shared the same tight friendship.

Every Saturday evening, our four pals went to a nightclub, then spent the rest of the week regaling us with their exploits from that evening. It was also important for them to hang out in the hippest spots of Strasbourg. For them, the main thing was to be elegant and profit fully from everything this short life had to offer, without allowing this to prevent them in any way from making their five daily prayers—a kind of minimum service they owed themselves and God. In any event, they considered religion to be a personal matter and after the "departure on the path of God" on which I had sent them, they never wanted to hear another word about it from me.

Even if they respected the people of the tabligh, or at least said they did, they found this movement too constraining, and they detested the Muslim look of the brothers in the projects: the hairy beards, Nike Air Maxes, chéchia, and the Pakistani outfits with the pants cut short at the ankles. They often said—and we argued this point with them—that the first thing the brothers of the tabligh should do if they wanted to attract people was to improve their appearance. They gently teased us when Majid and I, dressed for combat, showed up to make them do their *dahwa* (preaching). "Dress like everyone else, guys, and after we will argue. . . ." they would tell us. They considered Islam a simple religion whose life and spirit we were needlessly complicating.

Fayette was the most introverted of our little band of brothers. He was content to live in his own bubble and showed scant interest in the divergence of opinions that animated our evenings. "Being Muslim is one thing, but there is still everything else. . . ." he would say, suggesting that our lives promised to be long and full of uncertainties. Inevitably, a day would come when one grew up, found a job and a wife, left mama, and created one's own home. And in this little life that would only be built after constant effort, there was no guarantee of any truly satisfying period of happiness. These were his chief concerns. We were Muslims? Great! That did not give us any right, "but rather duties," he would conclude in a disillusioned tone.

Meanwhile, our mother continued to show evidence of much goodwill in order that our new piety could bloom. Without ever being asked, she began buying meat from the Muslim butcher and often encouraged me to bring my little brothers to the mosque because, as she liked to say, "they will have more success in life if they pray!"

Of all the members of this peaceful family, I was the most absolute in my commitment. But my state of mind was gradually changing, although nothing of this change was visible on the surface. While on the outside I seemed to be blossoming in my career as an activist preacher, I felt increasingly troubled on the inside. I had come down from a certain state of euphoria, the "beginner's enthusiasm" as Majid and I called it.

The first thing I found shocking was the tendency shown by numerous Muslim immigrants to associate together by nationality rather than by religious affiliation. This was true for the Moroccans and the Algerians, and turned out to be equally true for the Turks. I personally had been victim of uncalled-for words concerning my skin color on several occasions. The universalism and antiracism of Islam, although quite real, unfortunately turned into empty words in the mouths of many Muslims whose actions were quite contrary to these utopian ideals. This exacerbated nationalist spirit was particularly visible and appalling during the Aïd el-Fitr, the "little feast" that is celebrated at the end of Ramadan, and the Aïd el-Kebir, the "big feast" at which a sheep is sacrificed. Each community prayed in separate locations—at least the North Africans and Turks did. (There were not enough members of the other nationalities to have their own place for prayer.) Let's not even speak about the question of marriage, in which the parents' priority was finding a girl from their native land. . . .

Numerous stories circulated on this subject. Young men and women had been compelled to break with their families rather than renounce their love. Even in our own mosque, everyone remembered the bachelor brother of Senegalese origin whose merits, piety, and politeness had been highly praised by all the hajis. Once he had the misfortune to fall in love with the daughter of an elder of North African descent, which he did not trouble to conceal, almost all turned their backs to him and ostensibly refused to speak to him.

The adventure would have been of short duration if his passion had not been shared, but the young woman did—absolutely! After vainly trying to enter into the good graces of the young girl's parents, the two lovebirds decided to elope—the presence of two witnesses would be sufficient—before fleeing to the Parisian area. These dramatic denouements were quite common and sometimes led to catastrophe when the elder brothers became involved or when the specter of what the neighbors might say became too overwhelming for the families. Hadn't the Prophet Muhammad (PSL) fought against every form of segregation, whether based on social or ethnic origin? Wasn't Islam a religion without borders, intended for the whole of humanity and for every era? This whole issue left me perplexed and filled with sorrow. Fortunately, this racism was contested and rejected by the majority, but it was already deeply rooted in many minds.

I realized that my own vision of Islam, which I believed to be open-minded, was only a yoke that was beginning to fit on me too tightly. What I found especially wrenching was the fact that the tabligh, of which I had seen only the positive aspects and which had contributed greatly to my own blossoming, was in the process of becoming corrupted before my eyes. It too, by dint of promoting an ideal, had developed into small exclusionary groups that competed to display who was the most holy. This forced certain individuals—the allegedly truly good, committed, and activist Muslims—to the forefront to the detriment of others who were all equally good Muslims in reality, but believers who practiced their faith more discreetly.

The attitude of some was therefore colored by an insidious form of condescension that rendered dialogue increasingly difficult. The movement was used like a social escalator and certificate of excellence through which some individuals could find a more exalted kind of lifestyle than that available in their fairly mediocre, profane lives. The majority of the faithful, who were certainly as sincere as I was, were a thousand leagues from imagining what plots were being hatched in the wings. I observed all of this with disgust, but a part of me still refused to see the reality, so I kept my thoughts to myself. Furthermore, more and more young people were rallying to Islam through the perspective offered by this faction, and in my opinion, this was all that truly mattered. After all, my criticisms could only well be the product of an error of passing judgment.

But as more time passed, the very degrading feeling that I was regressing intellectually grew stronger. Some years earlier, Majid had given me, as a birthday gift when I turned eighteen, the dazzling *Niche of the Lights,* and I became an impassioned fan of its author, the Imam al-Ghazali, a great theologian of the Middle Ages. My raiding of the shelves of Muslim libraries was generally futile; except for a few rare mystical texts, all the books I found were overflowing with puerile rhetoric. I, who had been a zealous private-school scholar and philosophy student, had the growing impression that the Islam on which I was feeding by means of the tabligh was becoming more impoverished as my philosophical and rational knowledge continued to grow.

I also noted that a good many of my Muslim elders—although highly educated with many diplomas—metamorphosed into dull brutes when the subject was religion, as if the simple fact of mentioning Islam inhibited all their intellectual capabilities—whereas the example of an al-Ghazali should have increased them tenfold. Once they began talking about Islam, they seemed to be speaking as if on automatic pilot, mechanically reciting their catechisms with all critical spirit vanishing from their remarks.

I too, however, was trapped in this spiral, as an observer and as one implicated. This dualism was tearing me apart in such a way that I sometimes managed to convince myself that it was the devil personally forcing me to see all these shortcomings in order to distance me from the community. Thus reassured by my own blindness, I continued to lie to myself and kept up the pretense of seeing nothing. Obviously, this only accentuated my sense of uneasiness, and after a while, I believed I even had completely lost my footing. I participated less and less in the *khuruj* and spent almost no time with any of my Muslim brothers, only visiting the mosque for my five daily prayers. Every time a group came by to learn what was new for me (which is to say quite often) and to urge me to "depart," I made up some excuse to avoid this ordeal. Lying on these occasions only added to my feelings of guilt and confusion. It was during this time that I first attended a lecture by Tariq Ramadan* in Saint-Louis, not far from the border with Switzerland. I would later have dealings with him on a more personal basis in circumstances connected to my musical activities.

Over the course of the summer of 1991, our notoriety had spread far beyond the city limits. NAP had become the biggest rap group of the region, enjoying popularity (according to some of the local media) equal to that of Kat Onoma's rock group—who had national recognition and who had signed a contract with a major label. That summer we scoured the entire region of Strasbourg and the surrounding area for places where a group could perform, and one August night we finally had our inaugural performance. This was an open-air concert in Hautpierre in front of the local cultural center, Le Maillon, where we opened, before a tightly packed and enthusiastic crowd, for the Little, Parisian rap stars from the banlieue town of Vitry-sur-Seine. I was convinced that this was only the beginning and that we could go much further, that we had what it took to be a national group. A year later, we had succeeded in anchoring our notoriety a little deeper, and from Alsace to the Belfort territory by way of Lorraine and the Doubs, we were definitely the number one rap group. However, despite numerous attempts, we still had not managed to land a contract with a record company.

---

*[Tariq Said Ramadan is a Swiss Islamic scholar and theologian who believes that European Muslims need to establish a specifically European kind of Islam and advocates their integration into European society. He is the grandson of the Egyptian Hassan al-Banna—founder of the fundamentalist movement the Muslim Brotherhood. —*Trans.*]

However, I had fallen prey to what I considered to be a much more serious problem. My recent entry into music, which I believed to be incompatible with my religious activity—music is haram according to certain authorities—posed a cruel dilemma for me. Of course, all the members of the group accepted my religious enthusiasm, but they had all staked their futures on music. I held a central position in the group, and the fraternal bonds connecting me to each of the other members forbade me from acting egotistically.

I therefore continued to perform rap in much the same way that a patient follows the course of treatment for a shameful disease. I eventually constructed a rationale for my activity based on fairly twisted logic: the more quickly we advanced professionally and gained success, the more quickly I could retire and devote myself entirely to Islam. In the meanwhile, I led a double life of preacher and rapper—while pursuing my studies. I took scrupulous pains to ensure that, except for Majid, none of the people with whom I was involved spiritually were at all aware of my musical activity.

I even went deeper into the splitting of my personality and the torturous rationalizing that allegedly justified my conflicting activities. It was common in the projects that anyone who made a name for himself in this or that sector would be approached by the neighborhood bigwigs, who were always keen on finding new areas for investment. One of these big shots had displayed considerable interest in us, and after many hesitations on my part, I finally agreed to meet him, thinking that a helping hand would accelerate our climb and therefore permit me to disengage myself from my musical life all the more quickly.

For more than a month, in more or less secret meetings, I explained to him how the music industry operated and what its specific needs were, from management to production and self-promotion, including how records were released and even how concerts were organized. This interested him so much that at the end of our discussions, he offered to loan me the modest sum of fifty thousand francs at no interest. He explained to me that I should look at it as a little financial incentive because we deserved one, and because we came from the same neighborhood, and that we needed to stick together, and so on. I gave my verbal consent, and when he knocked at my door several days later to give me a small garbage bag containing two hundred bundles of francs, I grabbed the money like a terrified virgin prostituting herself for the first time. That evening in bed, I wept as if my heart were breaking, terrified by this little garbage bag filled with dirty money, which I had hidden beneath my clothing in the room's only dresser, which I shared with Bilal.

With money in hand, we could finally start our own independent label, which allowed us to produce our first singles ourselves, then our first album. This summer of 1994 was rich with promise. Suddenly, the three years of futilely going door-to-door from one Parisian record company to the next seemed far behind us. One of our tours even allowed us to meet Sulee B, the charismatic leader of the Little, with whom we had briefly crossed paths at the famous opening concert in Hautpierre. But at that time, the Little were already stars, whereas we were minor provincials just good enough to get the audience warmed up for the main event, and this context was not propitious for a true meeting of the minds.

To measure the importance of the Little, it should be emphasized that during this period this group was one of only five or six rap groups to have signed a record contract and thus been given the possibility of reaching a national audience. Their influence was the source for the emergence of an entire generation of artists and decision-makers at the heart of the French hip-hop movement and the record industry in general.

During this time, in which we were regularly descending upon Paris, by chance Bilal and Karim crossed paths with Sulee and Ronald, the duo of the Little, at the Gare du Nord [North Station]. Bilal wanted to accost them spontaneously, but Karim dissuaded him, saying that that attitude was not "worthy of someone of our rank." By targeting Bilal's ego in his argument, he had aimed accurately, and Bilal therefore did nothing when the two members of the Little brushed past him.

That evening, when returning to my cousin Frédéric's—where Bilal and I customarily stayed—Bilal told us of his adventure. I entered into a mad rage and swore to Bilal that if by some miracle *I* was lucky enough to encounter them, I would not display such misplaced pride. We had to do whatever it took to climb through the ranks, and I thought that Karim and Bilal had let a golden opportunity slip by.

The following afternoon, Bilal and I were making our way to the Place des Vosges in Paris for a meeting I had managed to obtain with someone at Virgin. The rather friendly assistant of one of the artistic directors welcomed us to her office and gave us her full attention, promising to pass our demo along to her boss. We thanked her without real conviction before leaving, and then started walking, with nothing to say to each other.

Just as we were about to descend into the first metro entrance we came across, Bilal stopped short for no apparent reason. "We should not go this way!" he said without looking back at me. I insisted we keep going all the same, but he would have none of it. We therefore headed toward another entrance to the Bastille metro station, the one that is right in front of the FNAC store dedicated exclusively to music. Hardly had we arrived at the entrance when who did we see rising out of the depths of the earth as if by magic? Sulee and Ronald, who were taking the stairs four at a time! My wish had been granted: here they were now, just in front of us! Completely determined not to let this unhoped-for chance slip through our fingers a second time, we approached them without hesitation, and I told them our story. Touched, they agreed to meet us several days later at their home in Vitry-sur-Seine, and we've been steadfast friends for ten years.

It was during this time that Nadir was released from prison and came back into my life. He had conscientiously climbed through the ranks of petty crime with flair before making his entrance into high banditry with honors. He had never lost his famous "golden hand" from the glorious pickpocketing era and had continued to exercise his talents in disciplines as diverse as car theft, cocaine dealings, and most of all, stick-ups. With a few others, Nadir had become a notorious figure to the police and the greatest criminal of our region.

One afternoon in the projects, our paths crossed by chance. We reminisced about the good old days together, and during our discussion, I became aware of how much I had matured since that time. I also grasped why Nadir had always been the better one of us: in his genre—a somewhat specialized one, it's true—Nadir was a sage.

The months that followed gave us numerous occasions to see each other again, learn to know each other better, and truly come to respect one another. One day when we were driving around in a car—I remember it particularly because a friend had lent us his 1970s-era, brown Citroën for the day—I suggested to Nadir that he become our manager. He did not hesitate very long, for once the initial surprise had passed, he realized that he had been offered a real possibility for rehabilitation. My offer was not innocent. I knew that his instincts, which had been honed in the world of the streets, would be of great use to us; all I needed to do was train him.

In the street, as in the music industry, sound business sense, determination, and aggressiveness—all preferably allied with wisdom—are excellent qualities to possess. Nadir had them all. We were on the point of releasing our first album nationwide, in partnership with one of the largest independent marketing groups of the time. They distributed rap artists like La Cliqua, Expression Direkt, and Ideal J. Nadir was thus the man sent by providence at a pivotal point in our career. As the perfect touch on top of this good news, he also became my friend.

My hidden financier continued to give me his support in the form of garbage bags filled with money. I pushed my existential doubts to the side and again "departed on the path of God." I was also most assiduous in attending lectures that had been organized throughout France by the UOIF,* most particularly those given by Tariq Ramadan. I was

*[The Union of Islamic Organizations of France. —*Trans.*]

frenetically doing all of this as a way of absolving myself, as when, with the Catholicism of earlier times, people went to confession in order to be able to continue sinning.

I was again living a life of complete paradox. This schizophrenia I thought I had bypassed by embracing Islam trapped me in a more subtle form. On the one hand there was music, which was my passion, and my ambiguous relationship with money, embodied by my secret financier. On the other hand, there was my status as a preacher of Islam, which declared both music and criminality haram. Where was the good? Where was the bad?

I was swimming in complete confusion and hated myself for not fully living up to the image I wished to have of myself. I had become a strolling lie, a chameleon. In order to avoid drowning once and for all, I made my excessive practice into a life buoy, taking as my model the renowned Tariq Ramadan, in whom I wished to see again the figure of Malcolm X. Every day, however, I had the impression of sinking deeper into the quicksand on which I had planted my tent all by myself. Even Majid, who had been my support for all those years, had retired from the NAP venture for reasons of religious conviction. For the first time, I found myself truly alone.

When our first album, *La racaille sort un disque* [The Riffraff Release Record], was finally available in the record shops of France and Navarre, it became a genuine hit. The objective of this album was, first, to show that youth from the ghetto could still accomplish something, and that we not only knew how to express ourselves but could even— what a surprise!—show proof of intelligence and profundity. *La racaille sort un disque* took back for our own purposes a term that had been used to stigmatize us and turn it into a title of glory—just as in another domain the most militant radicals of Africanness called themselves niggers and not blacks.

The national recognition we attained exceeded all of our hopes. We became stars of the ghetto. All the projects in France, and I say this with no exaggeration, knew NAP. On the heels of this success, Nadir organized a triumphal tour across France. And when our first video, "Je viens des quartiers" ["I Come from the Hood"], was aired on M6 and MCM, at a time when we were only known to our audience in the projects, this media coverage guaranteed us select display on the shelves of major stores. After seven years painfully laboring in the regional compost, the success of this first work made us one of the rare provincial groups, after the legendary IAM, to penetrate the national level.

Despite this liftoff, a number of other aspects of our lives had gone down the drain. My cousin Frédéric, who now called himself Aïssa, had eventually found the answers he was looking for by welcoming Islam into his life—radical Islam. He had married when barely nineteen, believing this to be an absolute necessity to become a true believer. He adopted this excessive approach to life in every area of his life and ended up becoming completely disconnected from the world.

He, who until that time had been keen on all of the latest forms of rap and regarded rap as the apple of his eye, took advantage of our visit to Plessis one day to give us his entire collection of original cassettes. Like Majid, Aïssa justified his attitude by explaining that music was potentially dangerous for our religious development. One needed to gradually free oneself from a passion that could prove to be destructive. His attitude was strongly inspired by the *salafis*—a strict and pietist movement that claimed descent from the legist Ibn Taymiya (1263–1328) and took its name from the first three generations of Muslims, which were considered an absolute model. Aïssa began spending time with this fundamentalist movement almost exclusively, and his rigid and intransigent behavior alarmed me. He was the complete opposite of the free and open Frédéric I had always known.

After a passage of time, my worries found confirmation in a sad and unusual fashion. Aïssa divorced his wife abruptly for obscure reasons and began drinking, first secretly, then out in the open. This was such a shock to me that I preferred to pretend not to notice, thereby allowing him to continue his descent into Hell.

When I later learned that he was hanging out in Paris and spent his days drinking himself senseless in the brothel bars of Pigalle, I tried to reason with him. He was still my cousin, no matter what, and I could not forget that our passionate discussions some years earlier had led to my own conversion. In the beginning, I was completely incapable of grasping how he could have made the switch from being a perfect Muslim to that of complete derelict without any transition, because I believed that Islam protected its faithful from going adrift in this way. In my still overly Manichean vision of the world, it was easier for me to see this as some form of divine punishment, but just what had he done that was so bad?

When Aïssa was reinstated in the group during the recording sessions for our first album, it was not rare for him to show up completely drunk. It was glaringly obvious, but I failed to understand until later that, like thousands of people in the projects who went from one extreme to the other, he was only expressing his existential distress about his inability to find a place in a world he did not understand and that appeared to not want him. What was he looking for specifically? What are all those drifting young people who commit suicide with the help of cans of high-proof beer and spliffs looking for?

My passion for school and studying had spared me from numerous traps, but essentially I was just as fragile as my cousin and ran the risk of toppling over at any moment. However, after a dark incident involving drugs in which Aïssa lost his best friend, he created a void around himself, refrained from touching even a drop of alcohol, and walled himself away in a muteness that he broke only when our musical obligations forced him to. A person still has to eat.

Our manager, Nadir, had been the architect behind the success of our first album, but the day inevitably arrived when his past life finally caught up to him. After serving a year of preventive detention, he was once again summoned to appear in court where, accused of armed robbery, he was given ten years of hard time. The verdict struck our musical and friendly venture like a thunderbolt. We were reeling. Nadir was our brother-in-arms, he represented a part of us; it was if we had all been found guilty. Furthermore, he was completely indispensable on the professional level.

At almost this exact same time, my youngest brother Stéphane—the one who had never seen our father—sunk into the most violent kind of criminal activity. He stayed out all night on a regular basis, hung around with the little thugs of the projects, smoked and drank himself into a stupor, and inevitably ended up in prison when he was still a minor.

Along with these personal misfortunes, the projects continued to produce their daily lot of tragedies, which affected friends and relatives; some of these tragedies dealt us dreadful blows. For example, there is the one that occurred the day we returned from a concert we had performed in Colmar. It involved a young man named Fouad—Moroccan by origin, a high school student without a stain on his record and an athlete who was never seen without a blazing smile on his face.

Earlier on that particular day he had seen, just like everyone else leaving the mosque at that same time, a mob that had gathered around an extremely violent scuffle between two guys. Pulled closer by curiosity, Fouad not only realized that one of the combatants was none other than his elder brother, but that he was also in an extremely disadvantageous position. Without stopping to think, Fouad blindly threw himself into the melee. No one really knows what happened next. Lost in the crush of the crowd, Fouad was stabbed beneath his armpit and collapsed to the ground. He was bleeding copiously but never voiced any complaint; he simply stared at the sky while he lay on the lawn.

My brother Fayette and Majid, who were present at the scene, immediately called for help, but it never arrived. There was a tendency for this to happen when it involved Neuhof. Several young men from the projects then decided to transport Fouad to the hospital themselves. Alas, he had already lost too much blood and fell into a coma when being admitted at the emergency room. He died several days later.

This was followed by the story of little Farouk, who was only thirteen or fourteen when he succumbed to a violent asthma attack and whose father, eaten away by guilt, asked me to attend the imam in his place during the mortuary washing of his son's corpse. When the imam executed these ritual ablutions on the lifeless body, one had the impression that little Farouk was just sleeping peacefully on that metal table. I can still see myself returning on the bus from the morgue with Farouk's clothes stuffed in an Auchan bag, staring blankly at the urban landscape that flowed by indifferently. His family and mine were close. This kid was someone I watched grow up, from the time he had been a little child.

Then there was the woman who lived in our building who was found hanged in her small apartment one day. She had taken her own life because she had no longer been able to tolerate the pain of exile and the daily sight of her daughters' disgrace; they had a reputation in the quarter for using their bodies as their sole means of expression.

Poverty was never a disaster for me because my mental life cast a veil over it that protected me. Even my Islamic faith, despite my strong egotistical tendencies, was permeated by this detachment. I hope I can say this without lying: I have the profound feeling of having always been sincere, and this is undoubtedly why I was able to pass so easily from one contradiction to the next. Each key moment of my life up to the present had been a rupture prompted by the death of someone . . . or of something inside of me.

This chain of misfortunes made me aware of the relativity of everything I had set up as absolute truth. The act of believing deeply (without ever proclaiming it openly) that we, the Muslims, were on one side, and the miscreants (the kufar), were on the other, had contributed to maintaining this duplicity in me. This constant discrepancy, this discreet and hypocritical distance with respect to suffering, made it obvious that, over time, all my actions, even when I thought they were pious, could only be resolved in paradox or by continuously pulling me to a lie.

I could clearly see that there was neither an "us" nor the "others," just men and women in quest of happiness. I strongly felt that all of us were only "one" and that any notion of a radical splitting of humanity into two camps was only a comforting lie. But I was not yet ready to carry this realization to its logical conclusion, and because I remained torn in this way—between a universalist ideal and a quotidian reality—I felt incapable of raising myself to a new level.

Islam seemed to have offered me some help at the beginning, but I now found myself with my back to the wall, having no greater confidence than I had at the start of my journey. Yet I had devoured all the books written by Tariq Ramadan, attended all of his lectures, and redoubled my efforts in the activities of the tabligh, despite my reservations. All this proved to be fairly fragile bandages, masking no shortage of open wounds.

Everything I had learned so fervently—a confused blend of authentic spiritual truths and moronic slogans—was of no help to me. My hunger remained unsatisfied. I would have loved to find contentment, as Majid did, in what we were offered, to intoxicate myself with the soothing words of brother Tariq, the exalted preaching of those with whom I "went out" from mosque to mosque across France, and the well-meaning and moralizing advice that was so generously bestowed upon us. I understood his faith, I understood it suited him, but it did me no good. This lifestyle had a hollow ring to my ears. My demand was deeper and more essential.

The crowning blow to all of this was that my "departures on the path of God" were also becoming promotional campaigns! From one day to the next, half of the young people we approached on the street foisted themselves on me to ask for my autograph. I no longer had any idea of where to stand, and it was a total fiasco for me until the day when the emir of our group took me aside in the mosque and gave me a long lecture. To recap it in a few words, he ordered me to cease all my rap activity because, according to him, music was a perilous threat to my Islamic practice.

To soften the harsh tone of his criticisms and threats of divine wrath, he also explained to me how he had been a huge fan of the American singer Barry White, but he had not hesitated to destroy all of his 33s for the cause of God. Since then, the emir said emphatically, things had only gone better for him. I then had to face the disapproving gazes of the members of the group, and perhaps it was this ordeal that left a most painful impression upon me. I asked myself if they might not be right, after all. It was impossible to reconcile two such conflicting activities any longer. This was my last "departure on the path of God."

While I was going through this grim period of doubt, the major label BMG signed us to a fabulous contract for our second album, which was entitled *La fin du monde* [The End of the World]. While we were recording it, I felt a pressing need to make my current activities relevant to my beliefs, and I immersed myself in reading al-Ghazali, al-Muhasibi, and even Ibn Ata Allah. Reading these works gave me access to another dimension of Islam, and the mystical themes they put into play resonated within me, as if I had studied them in an earlier life, even if I had no belief whatsoever in reincarnation! While pursuing the production of this album, I made a capital decision: never again would I be satisfied with a superficial religious attitude and never again would I artificially separate my artistic activity from my spiritual path. What remained unclear, however, was just how I was going to translate this resolution into practice.

It was during this period of self-questioning that I benefited from the visit of Tariq Ramadan to Strasbourg, where he was giving a seminar on Qur'anic exegesis. This was on a winter evening in 1998. I had already visited Lyon for discussions with Éditions Tawhid, the publishers of his books. As I had not gotten much of anything from my long discussions with them on the subject of music and its legitimacy, I wished to learn directly from Tariq Ramadan's own mouth what the man with such great influence over an entire Muslim generation in France thought.

We met with him at the home of Majid, accompanied by all the members of NAP and the imam from the mosque near the Strasbourg train station. Though our discussion was courteous and fraternal, his opinions were too broad to give me any satisfaction. As Western Muslim artists, he explained, we should buckle down and create an unprecedented art form that conformed to our Muslim faith. I agreed, but his words aroused no echo in me. I knew full well that nothing, in music as in other domains of art, was born spontaneously. All the contemporary trends, currents, and styles had a genealogy, and they fertilized each other a fortiori in this multicultural West. The recommendations of our supposed mentor could eventually be realized on the level of writing, our choice of themes, and even in vocal interpretation, but from the strictly musical point of view, his advice made no sense.

While tasting the delicious meal prepared for us by the woman who was now Majid's wife, I forced myself to smile between two mouthfuls of Coca-Cola, but my perplexity remained intact. Our discussion extended into dessert, and before leaving, brother Tariq assured us that he would listen carefully to our album and quickly give us his reaction. Spotting the persistent uneasiness visible in my eyes, he ventured the observation that my problem might come from the fact that my musical creations did not truly agree with my faith. These words froze my blood. What did he mean by that? Could he be right? And if this *was* the case, was he insinuating that I should get in tune with his interpretation of Islam? So what if I was deeply depressed, I still jealously guarded my freedom. I was asking for advice, not an ideological tutor.

The reaction to our record that he promised never arrived directly from him, but his entourage contacted us in order to set up a meeting with other Muslim artists facing the same concerns. This involved forming an artistic committee charged with making our records compatible with Islam. I refused to work with what I felt was akin to a board of censors: there was no chance that anyone could make me rewrite what had sprung straight from my heart in order to force it to fit inside some frame. I had come to them as a young musician in search of knowledge about the positions of the tradition we shared. In response, I received an invitation to accept a humiliating defeat I was not prepared for (like the Romans at Cadium) at the hands of a closed-loop system. I had come with my Muslim sincerity and humility and met an attempt to incorporate my itinerary into a power strategy.

All at once, my instinctive rejection of this kind of method freed me of the yokes I had personally placed over myself. My decision was also influenced by a similar encounter I had during this same time. I met Yusuf Islam—the English pop star who had been known as Cat Stevens before his conversion—during a lecture we gave in common on "art in Islam today." During our long conversation, he made the same speech to me that I had heard from Tariq Ramadan, and like the latter, he never responded to the album I sent him afterward.

Several months later, we left on a marathon tour with Sté and Oxmo Puccino (Parisian rap artists contracted with Delabel) through France and Switzerland. As our second album had attained real success, the concerts we performed were quite memorable. On several occasions, numerous individuals of all nationalities and both sexes came backstage to tell us how our songs had really shaken up and transformed their lives. Some had even entered the Muslim faith thanks to our intervention. Others told us that our texts had helped strengthen their roots in their own religion—Christian or Jewish—by showing them that religious questions were ultimately universal. This, we felt, was an incredible thing. They all came to thank us for what we had done for them or someone close to them. What a topsy-turvy world! Our raps and interviews were able to help perfect strangers put order into their lives, while our own lives (especially mine, as it appeared to me) were still, more than ever, definitely under construction.

Several weeks after this tour ended, the JMF (Jeunes musulmanes de France [Young Muslims of France]) invited us to give a concert in Nantes. This offer touched me enormously because despite the countless letters of protest if not outright threats they received urging them to cancel this event, they never ceded an inch and the concert took place. I had the intense feeling that I had found kindred spirits in them, and for that I will always be grateful.

It was on this occasion that I made the acquaintance of the president of the JMF at that time, Farid Abd al Krim, and especially the imam Tariq Oubrou, rector of the mosque of Bordeaux. This singular imam with exquisite manners and obvious sincerity had a huge effect on me, both with his personality and his words—especially his words. He regarded our activity as legitimate and even salutary. Although he was certainly a keeper of orthodoxy as a scholar, he spoke first and foremost as a shepherd of souls who paid attention to who we were and not some hidden strategy. Finally, a man of God who took an interest in us and our blossoming rather than trying to inculcate in us some prefab ideological diagrams ready to think! In a word, he trusted us. With him, I began to instinctively sense the possibility of a third way beyond that of a strict and idiotic practice and that of pure and simple apostasy.

I would later have a number of additional enriching conversations with this imam. I remember the day when he told me that a society could not consist entirely of theologians. This simple statement, no matter how obvious it seems in hindsight, touched me to the core. I had been stressed out—like the majority of Muslims in a society where they are the minority—from the perpetual anxiety of wondering what was licit or illicit. I never really knew what was halal or haram. This was an anxiety that engendered guilt because it gave one the feeling of never living up to one's faith and created an obsession to show perfect respect for the orthodox rules—without ever managing to, of course, because of the contingencies of real life.

But here was the answer: not all of us are doctors of the law! And we did not all need to become that, but rather each find our own path with the singular predispositions that have been given to us. Does not the Qur'an say: "Allah never imposes anything upon a soul that is beyond its abilities"? And did not the Prophet Muhammad (PSL) state: "Make things easy, do not make them difficult"? This evidence, which may appear banal, was extremely liberating for me because it came from the mouth of a doctor of the faith.

I had given a great deal of thought to marriage since entering Islam, but I still had not found the "sister" with whom I had enough in common to take such a step. Since I had become a member of the Islamic faith, I had not touched any women at all, as advocated by the religion (outside of marriage). Honestly speaking, I had not felt any imperious need to do so, constantly occupied as I was with my many activities and my wild internal imaginings.

The time for marriage eventually arrived, but this decision had nothing motivating it, by which I mean that it was not inspired by love. The young woman whom I was preparing to wed was a childhood friend I saw from time to time. After several years, both of us observing that we were still single, the subject came up and we said: "Why not?" We were already engaged in a certain way due to the fact our parents had already agreed on the marriage arrangements.

However, shortly after the release of our first album, I went to visit Sulee one day with Majid—who was madly in love and on the verge of getting married. It was then that Sulee introduced me to Naouale, whom I had never met before. Even before I shook her hand, I had immediately fallen head over heels in love with her. Of course, I acted as if she had hardly any effect on me. I even shared with her the fact, as if to gag my heart, that I was on the verge of getting married.

Of Moroccan origin, she had a very pretty face with a childlike freshness and magnificent wavy brown hair that rippled. She told me that she had played violin since the age of twelve, that she was going to law school, was single, and lived in her parents' apartment in a project in Bobigny with her nine brothers and sisters. She was just starting her career as a singer, and it had been less than a year since Sulee had been composing music for her; already her talent was evident on the demos. When I heard her first songs, I was convinced that she was on her way to becoming a great artist.

Naouale was profoundly religious. She had been praying since her earliest childhood, and her parents had given her a perfect education, despite the hardships of life in the projects of the suburbs. Cultivated and intelligent, she had a passion for classical music and for mystical literature and poetry. She had everything going for her: beauty, elegance, intelligence, and talent. She was blessed, and I was totally under her spell.

I took advantage of my frequent trips to Paris, necessitated by my musical activity, to visit Sulee's home every time Naouale was there. I had gotten into the habit of discussing hip-hop and especially Islam with her; they presented many opportunities for sounding her out and getting to know her better. It was futile to try and clear my mind; her image haunted my thoughts constantly. This situation became increasingly troublesome given the fact that I was supposed to be getting married to someone else in a few months time. . . .

It was then that I made an important decision. If the first woman to come along—even if Naouale was exceptional—was able to distract me from the woman with whom I was planning to spend the rest of my days, then I had a real problem on my hands! This clearly had not been obvious to me, and was even less obvious to her, to say nothing of our parents, who had already planned out the wedding ceremony to its smallest detail, determined the number and birth order of our children, and so on—but the die was cast. I broke the engagement once and for all. From that point on, we went our separate ways, and she heard no more from me nor I from her.

Should I propose to Naouale now that I was free of any conjugal commitment? And what would happen if she had no interest in me? I found what comfort I could in the thought that I had nothing to lose, and so on the eve of NAP's departure for our first big tour, I wrote Naouale a long letter in which I told her everything she meant to me. Several weeks later on my return to Strasbourg, I found a letter waiting for me on my bed. It was from her. I read it at least ten times in succession. In it she said that barely had someone told her about me, then she had met me in the flesh, but before doing that, she had fallen in love with me. The thunderbolt that had struck me was reciprocated by her.

We were married a few years later, but not without going through some difficulties, tears, and sacrifices, but "God is with the patient." Our love was stronger than the borders drawn by men. We initially lived in exile here and there before settling in Thiais in the Val-de-Marne region. And it was precisely in this town in the southern suburbs of

Paris that a year after we moved in I found myself standing helplessly by, waiting for my wife to give birth.

Somebody came to hurriedly ask me to come while she was being transferred to the birthing room. I slipped into the scrub shirt someone held out to me and joined her there. Her contractions were already quite strong, and I could read the martyrdom she was undergoing on her face. I remained constantly by her side, holding her hand. "A woman is better than a man!" is what I decided to always think from then on. A woman is infinitely stronger than a man. Guys can swell their biceps, spill their own blood or that of another, but that is not at all comparable to the courage of a woman, and especially a woman in labor.

Naouale appeared to be suffering atrociously to me. During one spike of pain, she yelled at me: "Do something!" The ridiculous male condition . . . . I answered her: "Breathe," and immediately felt like an even bigger idiot. I think this was the moment I really began to panic. I barely had time to tell myself "Get a grip on yourself!" before the anesthesiologist made me leave the room telling me: "This is going to take fifteen minutes. Epidural." I returned to the waiting room, where other future papas like me were also panicking.

The answering machine on my cell phone was chock full; everyone wanted news. I called my mother first, only to hear her tell me: "Everything is going to work out well, think of God. . . ." I heard something essential in her voice, the reason why she had always forgiven me, and indeed forgave everyone, even Stéphane. Even when he pulled the craziest stunts, even when he got out of prison, even when he returned home in the evening completely stoned on shit and alcohol.

I now got it. I now understood that being a woman is not a walk in the park. That being constantly belittled, disparaged, held up for ridicule with a glance, a word, or a smutty innuendo, was quite simply intolerable. Man grants himself strength and power, which works out quite nicely—for him! Out of love, my mother had tearfully left her family, her friends, and her country to disembark in a country she absolutely hated in the beginning and in which she next found herself alone, with no job and several children to raise. Yet no one ever heard her complaining. Even when beset by the worst crises, she was always able to find the strength within to not give in.

Equally important, she still managed to inculcate her values to her children. Thus armed with the love of a mother against the pressures of the street, we all had been able, despite everything, to pull ourselves out of the dead end that the street offered. She had spontaneously succeeded in holding her own against her personal demons where many men have been defeated, or where many men only succeed after a long life spent painfully owning up to their mistakes. How many men can be both father and mother to their child? Out of necessity, my mother, like countless other mothers around the globe, was able to perform this dual role. I love my mother.

And what can I say about Naouale, who courageously stood up to her family (although her love for them was as strong as ever) because of her love for me, and who then did everything in her power, braving humiliation, to win back the love of each of them by dint of patience and affection. . . ?

I remained that way, as if I were floating in the void. I was beside myself with love for my wife and my mother while my head was boiling with ideas. Then I was called back, and like an automaton, I rushed into the room, where everything speeded up. More than four hours had sped by in less than a second. I was in a daze. I have never fainted in my life, but it was a near thing when I first saw his glistening little head. I burst into a flood of tears like a kid. Naouale and the little one were radiant.

"Paradise is found beneath the feet of your mothers," says the Prophet (PSL).

FOUR

TOWARD THE UNIVERSAL

All I need is Love to be able to live as a free man
To remove the shackles of material life
To get rid of the superfluous and go toward the essential
Build solid one-to-one relationships
Each day tear away a bit more of the veil of appearance
All I need is Love to know myself and then know others
To grasp that we are all only one despite how many we are
in number
And see that the many in the end turns us into shadow
FROM THE SONG "THE LANGUAGE OF THE HEART"

It had already been several years since I had first become interested in Sufism, the mysticism of Islam. In the beginning, one of the brothers who took part in the teaching circle at the neighborhood mosque had spoken to me, on his return from a trip to Damascus in Syria, of a pious visit that he had made to the mausoleum of Ibn Arabi there. I did not then know what a "pious visit" was or who Ibn Arabi was, and I did not say anything to him in response. All of this brought to mind superstitious actions that were more or less contrary to the spirit of Islam.

Nonetheless, I was intrigued, enough so that his words etched themselves permanently into my memory. I had then purchased books on Sufism, bearers of a spiritual breath that was completely different— more ample, liberated, and profound—than what had been passed off to me as spirituality. Almost despite myself, this literature sustained me during those years spent under the aegis of the tabligh, the UOIF, and Tariq Ramadan. I was a big reader and many times found myself spending afternoons, even whole days, among the bookshelves of the FNAC. I had then often promised myself that one day I would buy a tome I saw there and coveted. The size of a paving stone, the cover bore, in addition to the face of a venerable black man with blue eyes clad Muslim style, a double title: *Amkoullel, l'enfant peul* [Amkouelle, the Fulani Child] and *Oui mon commandant* [Yes Sir, Commander] by Amadou Hampaté Bâ.

Finally, as I said earlier, Majid gave me a text by al-Ghazali as a gift for my eighteenth birthday, and during this same period, I had stumbled across the spiritual figure of Abd el-Kader in my reading. To my great surprise, I discovered that this great figure of the Algerian resistance against the French armies had also been a great Sufi and sublime mystical poet, the author of many fundamental works. Even better, he had been initiated as a Freemason during his forced stay in France and was buried, per his express desire, in Damascus near the tomb of Ibn Arabi, whom he considered his teacher despite the centuries separating them.

The concept of Islam carried by this path stressed that the most formidable battle to be waged, the *djihad al-nafs,* "jihad of the soul" or "major jihad," was the one that an individual waged against his own ego, which served as a screen between his deeper self and the divine. "He who knows his soul, knows his Lord," is how it is expressed in a hadith of the Prophet (PSL). After al-Ghazali, I had discovered a man he had considered one of his teachers, al-Muhasibi, whose name means "the one who demands explanations from himself." I liked this idea: instead of pointing an accusatory finger at others, it was necessary to challenge ourselves.

During the recording of *La fin du monde,* I feverishly plunged into these books, which gave me a hint of another Islam. Then, one fine morning, Mohammed, the founding member of NAP, who, like me, was deeply committed to a spiritual quest, but was much more serene in his pursuit of it, brought me a book that he had devoured the night before, *Traces of Light* by a certain Faouzi Skali. This small book was able to enlighten me as none before. I finally grasped that my Islam of the suburbs was actually a religiosity responding to the mental state of the French ghetto, but that it was also only a suburb of Islam. It remained on the periphery, sometimes even touching trouble spots but never reaching the heart—the spiritual and universal core of Islam.

I was enthused by this Sufi literature that sometimes shook me up so much that I wept. But I remained convinced that it was no longer possible to live this kind of spiritual experience, that no initiatory path still existed in our age. I believed this until I bought the autobiographical work by Amadou Hampate Bâ, about which I spoke earlier. I discovered, to my stupefaction, that not only had he followed a teacher from his early youth, but also that he had subsequently become a great master himself. Now, if Amadou Hampete Bâ had died in 1991, his legacy should still be living in the person of his successor or in some structure. This convinced me to research the matter further, and I finally stumbled upon the address of their brotherhood in a book! I became like a madman. I became absolutely obsessed with making contact with this order, the Tijaniya *Tariqa* (Brotherhood), whose motherhouse I had learned was in Fez, Morocco. I immediately made the decision to go there the following August.

The intuition of something beyond the immediate reality, the wings behind the stage where the meaning of the world was in play had, until this time, remained purely an act of faith for me, and this only fed my dissatisfaction. Expanding the field of my religious education had been in vain; the source of being still remained hidden away there without my ceasing to believe in its meaning. My actions, my attitudes, and my frustrations only definitively formulated one major question out of all those posed to me by life: who did this meaning veil from me?

This intuition, that something resembling plenitude existed beyond the veil, was something I had always felt. It had manifested, for example, in the inner upheaval I had experienced at the death of Hubert, and in my first Sufi readings. These experiences had made me let go and open myself to the real, to a degree that was more profound than what I had experienced through criminality and the projects, the tabligh, and the lectures of Tariq Ramadan. I felt it now, and the Sufis only confirmed what I was feeling: everything I had lived, up to the present, including my wanderings in the maze of institutions and ideologies boasting their Islamic identity, including even rap and my life as an artist, were only veils in comparison to my personal essence, that profound source to which I had to climb. This inextinguishable quest for the meaning I felt was nothing other than the echo in me of his call, just as it had been sung during the Middle Ages by the great Sufi poet, Ibn Arabi:

> Listen to me, dearly beloved!
> I am the Reality of the world,
> The center of the circumference,
> I am the parts and the whole. . . .
> Dearly beloved,
> So often I have called you,
> And yet you have not heard Me!
> So often I have revealed Myself to you,
> And yet you have not seen Me!
> So often I have made myself richly fragrant,
> And yet you have not smelled Me.
> Delicious food,
> And yet you have not tasted Me.
> Why are you unable to reach Me
> Through the objects you touch?
> Or breathe Me through sweet scents?
> Why do you not see Me?
> Why do you not hear Me?
> Why? Why? Why?

The very same night that I decided to go to Fez, a show about this great city of Moroccan history was aired on television. I asked Bilal to tape it for me because I had already made plans to attend a series of lectures organized for three evenings at the great mosque of Strasbourg on the theme of . . . Sufism. The two lecturers had already gotten well into their talks when I entered the jam-packed hall. They were complete strangers to me; I later learned they were Eric Geffroy, assistant professor at Strasbourg University, and Cheikh Bentounes, spiritual leader of the al-Alawiya Brotherhood.

I was struck to see that the majority of the audience consisted of people I had more or less run into at the mosques and who I knew to be hostile to Sufism. The two speakers were able to express their positions tranquilly during the time they held the floor, but things turned sour when the question-and-answer period began. The audience was in a state of peculiar excitement. Incomprehension bordering on hatred was motivating the majority of those picking up the microphone.

The speech of a young blond-haired convert with light-colored eyes, whom I knew from having spent time in the great mosque, was particularly virulent. He grew red with rage when he expressed his profound disagreement with even the name "Sufi." He declared that, given the fact we were all Muslim, the wish to distinguish oneself in this way from the rest of the community smacked of pride from the start and could only lead, over time, to a certain *fitna* (discord). He then noisily left the hall accompanied by a dozen or so people who were equally enraged as he.

I remained at the exit with some of my fellow faithful, but soon unpleasant remarks began flying thick and fast: "What a lot of nonsense!," "In any case that was all just cult stuff. . . ," "Why were those guys invited to speak, when there are much more serious things going on in Palestine and Chechnia, while they just spout their idiocies at us . . . ?" I had heard enough and snuck out at the first opportunity. The other two evenings took place in a much more agreeably calm environment, but it should be said that the audience was increasingly smaller.

The great Sufi mysticism, in which Muslim culture achieves its fullest flowering, had no visible echo or credibility in the projects.

Several weeks went by before I remembered the show on Fez that Bilal had taped for me. My disappointment upon seeing it—it was a tourist documentary on the new and old medinas—transformed into a feverish excitement when I caught the name of the anthropologist who narrated from time to time: Faouzi Skali! It was the author of *Traces of Light,* the book that had made such a huge impression on me . . . and I had thought it to be the work of an obscure dervish dead for several centuries! I had made my decision to go to Fez on the faith of a vague address dug out of a book, but here I had proof that a living Sufi was residing there!

From this moment, things seemed to start moving faster and faster. Several days later at the Place de l'Etoile, my path crossed that of a good friend of Moroccan origin who, after working as the director of the social and cultural center of Neuhof for almost ten years, now worked at the Strasbourg city hall at the side of Catherine Trautmann. He calmly told me that he had just launched a program he called the twin city program, which united Strasbourg, "the capital of Europe," with the city of Fez, which had been declared a "patrimony of humanity" by UNESCO [The United Nations Educational, Scientific, and Cultural Organization].

Two weeks later, while I was visiting Paris, I received a call from my friend Rachid Benzine, a teacher who had hosted NAP when he was producing a television show about the banlieues for Channel Five. I loosely shared my plan of going to Fez with him, and before I could explain my motivation for going there, he offered to give me the contact information "for a guy there who has written quite a bit on this subject, and who you will be able to ask all the questions you want." This individual was, of course, Faouzi Skali. And after I returned to Strasbourg, where Bilal and Mohammed announced to me that they had been loaned a minivan for most of the summer by the social center and they had chosen Morocco as their destination, there was no room in my mind for any lingering doubt.

I had declined Majid's offer concerning a trip to Damascus, but he had already made too many commitments to follow me to Fez. The idea that one of us would be going to the Middle East while the other was heading to North Africa had something seductive about it, and he decided to go there with his family for a month before making any final decision about a longer stay there. We parted from one another not sharing the same frame of mind. He was directed toward the acquisition of everything forming the exterior sciences of Islam—jurisprudence, dogma, and so forth. I, on the other hand, was leaving to travel toward a horizon that was just as Muslim, but more "spiritual." I wished to follow my course as a disciple, while he wished to follow his as a scholar. Despite everything, we would remain the best of friends, and we promised to share our experiences when we got back.

While crossing through southern Spain, my thoughts were stirred by Islamic Spain and by Ibn Arabi as I reflected on the unforgettable portraits he had drawn of the Sufis of Andalusia. Soon, we found ourselves on a quay in Málaga, waiting for the boat whose arrival would signal the beginning of the crossing through my being. The subtle overlapping of tradition and modernity, and the legendary hospitality of Morocco's people, make it a marvelous country. But despite the beauty that welcomed us and the keen emotions that possessed me when I set foot for the first time on Muslim soil, I was not really present. Only Fez occupied my mind, and the only value I saw in the towns we drove through after landing in Tangiers was that they brought me closer to my destination.

When we finally arrived in a Fez that had been set aglow by the setting sun and was vibrating to the call of the muezzins, I felt like I had reached the Promised Land. After spending the night in the neighboring village of Bahlil, our very first stop was a visit to the imam of Neuhof. He was also spending his vacation in his native city and offered to accompany us to the *salat jumuha* (Friday prayer) at the famous Qarawiyyin Mosque before taking us on a visit to the old medina.

While there, he took us to the mausoleum of Moulay Idriss, patron saint and founder of the city, then to the mosque of Ain al-Khail, where the omnipresent Ibn Arabi had gone through several major stages of his spiritual itinerary. I was as excited as a child at finding myself "for real" in these places that were charged with history and spiritual symbols and that provided a living framework of stones, people, and landscapes for the adventures I had read in all of his books.

After accompanying the imam back to his home, I insisted to the others that we go back to the old city so that I could visit the Tijaniya *zawiya,* but no one wanted to come with me. Some of my companions then decided to visit their families, while the rest wanted to go to the souk. Even our guide preferred visiting the souk over driving me to the zawiya. This day, like the following, something happened to prevent me from making the only visit that mattered to me. One morning, I decided to telephone Faouzi Skali, and after a more-than-warm welcome over the phone, he invited all six of us to dine with him at his house that very evening.

This anthropologist was around forty and had been educated in Paris. He taught at the École Normal [Teacher's College] of Fez and also directed the famous international festival of sacred music of the world held in Fez. He welcomed us with such warmth and hospitality that it was as if we were old friends. As the "little" Ahmed noted to me (Ahmed was a young man from the projects we had dragged along on our Moroccan excursion who, in fact, was over six feet tall and weighed over two hundred pounds), Faouzi Skali was incredibly zen! He expressed himself in a gentle and even tone, and all his gestures were of a hieratic slowness but not at all pretentious or fake.

This same evening, he was also entertaining some friends—all natives of Provence and southern France—who were already present when we entered the living room. The sight of these six white Muslim guests truly surprised me. It was not because I did not know other white Muslims, but these individuals were unique. In fact, the converted from the projects often had the same profile. They were extremely dogmatic and extremely partial to the Muslim sartorial fashion of folklore: they wore a turban on the head and had long beards and djellabas. Furthermore, in the opposite direction, one found the vexing tendency for the young of Africa or North Africa to strive to be more royal than the king and to think that integration had to occur through a denial of their roots. Of course, all the whites did not systematically adopt this same attitude, but many fell into this shortcoming, some even going so far as to suddenly break with their own families, who they now considered to be infidels.

This evening, in contrast, the friendly and ordinary whites who were present were not distinguished by any outer signs, or any mimesis, whether sartorial or of another variety. There was one other surprise: never in our conversation did they start preaching or criticizing French society or Western culture as "decadent and impious," whereas this had been a frequent attitude among the converted whites of the projects I had contact with.

After a Moroccan-style meal, which is to say it was more than plentiful, I bombarded Faouzi Skali with a series of questions that had been burning my lips since our arrival, and he graciously accommodated me. The uncertainties and anxieties that had collected over my solitary, doubt-filled nights finally found a way to openly express themselves, and he responded with a broad-mindedness the likes of which I had never encountered. While listening to him, I had the singular sensation of always having known what he was telling us!

At the root of my spiritual quest was the doubt that Christian dogma had been unable to soothe. The external Islam transported by the tabligh had then provided me nourishment with definitive and clear-cut answers, but this had only reinforced my ego with an armor of certainties. In a discourse entirely structured by the halal/haram dichotomy, the morality being offered to me was a form of nonthinking, with an accusatory finger pointed perpetually at the works of others. In this looking-glass world, I thought I was profound when I was superficial and I stuck my heart between the folds of my brain—without doing anything else to help it function properly as the level of the preaching was so low.

A Muslim practicing in pure orthodoxy, this man placed his entire teaching on a universal plane that dissolved, as if by magic, the black-and-white vision of the world that I had been taught. "In the depths of every individual," he said, "there is a profound secret, a pact that binds him or her beyond time and place to the essence of Being. The Qur'an reminds us that before souls took form on this earth, they all bore witness by direct contemplation of his Divine Lordship. It is by virtue of this knowledge present in each of us—even, paradoxically, without us knowing—that prophets and spiritual teachers come to us."

From time to time, he took a break to grab an orange from a basket of fruit. "The first teachers of the Way were therefore the prophets," he continued, while slowly peeling an orange. "And as the foremost, the first, among them—Adam. Muslim tradition insists in his repentance after the fall and the divine forgiveness that permitted him to regain the primordial dignity of which he had been stripped for a time. The essential nobility of Adam stems from the fact that he received the 'Mind of God' within—by virtue of which the angels must prostrate themselves before him. He is God's representative (*khalifa,* caliph) on earth. He is the mirror in which the divine Reality manifests. It so happens that whatever can be said about Adam is also valid for all of his descendents, for all the individuals of the only human race inherited his holy spirit, whatever their sex, race, or tradition."

I was bathing in an atmosphere of sweetness and honey. He then spoke to us about the prophets and especially about the spiritual teacher. Never could I have imagined that the master-student relationship could be so light and so unrestrictive—while being so structured. "Your teacher is not the one from whom you hear speeches," he said, quoting his own teacher, "but the one whose expression guides you, whose spiritual attitude penetrates you. He is not the one who directs you through words, but who transports you by his spiritual state. Your teacher is the one who frees you from the prison of the passions to introduce you into the home of the Teacher of worlds—which is to say God. He is the one who never ceases to polish the mirror of your heart so that the lights of Your Lord may shine there. He admits you into the light of the divine presence and tells you: 'Here you are at the home of Your Lord.'"

For him the teacher was the indispensable companion, thanks to whom the disciple can move beyond all his illusions and pseudo-knowledge to attain true knowledge, that which is made "by" and "within" God.

A memory of a story came to mind that a teacher had told us one day at the mosque for our edification as well as to inculcate in us absolute obedience to the group leader. Here is a brief version of the tale, whose exotic nature was surely intended to touch *us* in particular, insofar as three of the five young people present were African. A group of tabligh brothers had "departed on the path of God" in a remote region of sub-Saharan Africa. Night had fallen without any mosque or village nearby, and they were forced to sleep out under the stars. They had also been wandering all day with empty bellies so that when they found two baby elephants sleeping in a clearing, one of the brothers suggested they make them their dinner. Only the emir showed patience and attempted to convince the others that perhaps another solution would make itself known with the morning light.

Ignoring him, the others went ahead in obedience with their wishes, and the emir alone remained with his belly empty. However, when they were woken up in the middle of the night by the furious mother elephant, she trampled them all except for the emir. I had encountered this story in the context of the tabligh. The movement used it as an ideological tool in a way that was all the more subtle as it accompanied the Muslim's first act of faith, "submission" to one who exceeds him.

But one day when I had my nose buried in a collection of Sufi tales, I found this same story word for word and realized that the fundamental necessity for "obedience" had been led astray. It was in Sufism that I was able to grasp the true nature of this value: one must "submit" to one's own liberation and not be free while still inside one's own prisons. True humility involves discernment, intelligence, and decision. A spiritual teacher is never an intellectual leader or fine speaker, but someone who nourishes you with his spiritual flow. By mentioning the relationship he maintained with his teacher, Faouzi Skali introduced me to this dimension of a heart-to-heart relationship.

Since my childhood in Neuhof, whether at school or in the street, I had always occupied the position of the leader, the independent ringleader who influences without being influenced. This haughty figure crumbled away, and I realized that during all this time where I thought I was superior to others, I was only looking for myself in my reading or in an interpretation of Islam that I believed to be the only possible one—to the extent that I had convinced myself it was Islam itself. In reality, the preacher was no different from the criminal; I had only been wrestling on the surface of myself, seeking to flee what, in the depths of my being, exceeded me. I had always been proud and believed myself to be more intelligent than everyone else, and here I found a magnificent ignorance opening within me.

Faouzi Skali continued:

"Ordinary life for man involves the loss of his spontaneous nature, what in Arabic is called the *fitra,* and leads him to don social masks that are the expressions of values imposed by the outside world. According to the Qur'an, in his virgin, primordial nature, man spontaneously conforms to Divine Law and therefore to his inner norm. In the state of fitra, man acts in spontaneous coordination with the truth he carries inside, he acts in conformance with and under the impetus of his essential being. But when man loses this fitra, his state of being is no longer found within, but depends on the standards and opinions imposed on him by others; he is dependent on how others 'look' at him. The commitment of the disciple to the path of initiation consists of a growing awareness of the divine 'gaze,' which transcends that of men and focuses upon the inner life of the individual beyond all social roles. As one hadith says: 'Allah looks not at your shapes or your actions, he looks at what you hold in your hearts.' It is to the degree man acts for God, which is to say, to the degree he conforms to his true nature and is not uniquely based on how he expects others to view him, that determines if he becomes a monotheist within and distances himself from the hidden polytheism that consists of associating the 'gaze' of God with that of other men."

What a definition of monotheism! What joy it gave me to finally be able to combine rigor and freedom! Until this day, I had only been Muslim on the outside, for in my heart I had continued to prostrate myself before the idols of glory, reason, money, and fear. During this night, far from home, I finally awoke to myself. I had entered this living room as a sleepwalker, and the murmur of these worlds allowed me to guess what waking could be. The questions of reputation or image in the projects, of halal or haram in the mosques, even heaven or hell, were all reduced to nothing when it was a question of simply being.

When my eyes caught sight of a road sign announcing "Strasbourg—15 km," I realized that despite all that I had experienced, I had never actually set foot in the Tijaniya zawiya. Staring blinking at the nocturnal parade of trees, I mulled over the discussion that we had had in Faouzi Skali's living room. When I asked him what the definitive definition of love was, he quoted Djalal ad-Din Rumi, the founder of the Mawalwiya Brotherhood, the famous whirling dervishes: "Love is like a flame; when it enters the heart of the disciple, it burns everything, all that remains is God."

He then quoted more words from his teacher to me: "Love is the crown of all actions." For the professor, love was the central axis of all Muslim spirituality, if not all true religion. He held it as the most interior element of experience, only known to one who had tasted it: all spirituality was experience of divine love. At my request, he had gladly written his address for me, in case other questions came to me. He had been personally following a spiritual path for many years, which he had mentioned in passing during our discussion. I wished he had extended himself further on this subject because I was burning to ask him one sole question: "What must I do to enter the path to which you belong?" But my courage failed me, and I assumed that such an impatient request would have automatically disqualified me.

Majid and his little family returned from Syria several weeks after our return. His trip had dispelled his doubts, and he had made the decision to leave for Damascus next year. He did exactly this one year later, and while he was disappearing on the escalator taking him to the departure gate in Roissy,* I asked myself if I was doing the right thing by remaining in France.

Events over the next few months followed one another in quick succession. We were all more or less broke, and making a new album would undoubtedly help pull ourselves out of this jam. But because Nadir had been incarcerated again, the management of our company, which had coproduced *La fin du monde* with BMG, was in a state of chaos, and I had been forced to take over sole responsibility for it despite my lack of experience. If we wanted to benefit from any substantial financial advances, we would have to dissolve the contractual relationship between NAP and our production company and sign directly with BMG. What seemed simple on paper proved to be of exhausting complexity.

After protracted negotiations and countless days in the studio making demos, the major label finally agreed to sign us to a contract, but our artistic concerns were only just beginning. Up to the present time, being our own producers had given us the luxury of never owing explanations to anyone. Now that we were BMG artists, we could no longer work as we thought best, and every new piece we put together had to first be submitted to our artistic director, then validated by the CEO himself. I was so obsessed with these concerns that my spiritual quest had slipped

---

*[Roissy is the site of the Charles de Gaulle Airport outside Paris. —*Trans.*]

to the background, although it had now been two years since our return from Morocco. I was therefore partially absent from myself when I had to leave for New York to mix our album *À l'interieur de nous* [Inside Us] with Sulee, who had written almost all of our music.

I always felt somewhat peculiar in airplanes because Hubert died in one. I had never truly gotten over it, the pain had simply dissolved in the river of time. Four days after our arrival, we were in the studio. Prince Charles Alexander, all smiles, stood behind the recording console, his head, neck, and shoulders swaying to the beat of the rhythm and bass of the piece that was playing. "You're crazy," he said in English, never losing his smile, "the French are never going to get this!"

In the sound engineer milieu of the United States, Prince Charles was a star. During the '80s, he had been a member of a P. Funk group—a kind of psychedelic funk with heavy bass and synthesizers made famous ten years earlier by groups like Funkadelic or Parliament and artists like George Clinton or Bootsy Collins—before becoming the first engineer of black sound. This man, who had contributed to the success of artists like P. Diddy (Puff Daddy), Mary J. Blige, The Notorious BIG, or even French musicians like IAM, had agreed to work on our album for two reasons: having previously worked with Sulee, he held him and his talent in high esteem, and he found our album "terrific!"

Leaving Sulee to get his fill of videos on BET (Black Entertainment Television), I returned to our hotel on foot. The immense, compacted crowds, the stupefying buildings, the limousines, the yellow taxis, the noise, all of the elements of a city that television has made familiar to us, awoke in me a disagreeable sensation of foreignness. It was as if the city smashed me flat and rejected me. The Latino porter saw me come in but paid me no attention, as he had already been snagged by the promise of hefty tips by the people with heavy suitcases following me into the hotel. I went to the window, hoping to catch a glimpse of the sky, but saw only a naked wall. Every detail of New York life caused me to tremble, and I grasped nothing of what was happening to me.

This sense of malaise only intensified. At the studio, I no longer heard anything, neither the pieces nor what Sulee or Prince Charles was saying to me, and even less the words of the artistic director, who had just arrived from France. In this city that resembled a huge company in which everyone worked to feel alive, I had the impression of being the only person doing nothing, and this caused me to suffer. One night when I awoke with a start and was surprised to find tears on my pillow, I made the decision to write Faouzi Skali a long letter as a call for help. I asked if I could meet his spiritual teacher, the one about whom he had said nothing that memorable evening in Fez but who permeated all his words and gestures. I wanted his teacher "to take me by the hand for God."

When I returned home to Thiais, every morning I would go down to collect the mail, feverishly hopeful but always in vain. Perhaps I had explained myself poorly? Perhaps, finally, I was too far from corresponding to the profile of a future disciple? Perhaps I had simply mailed my letter to the wrong address? Or perhaps the letter had gotten lost in the American postal system—something that seems to happen frequently? Should I write him a second letter? Yes? No? I was caught in the snare of this anxiety when one evening Naouale told me that while I was out a certain Fabrice had telephoned on behalf of Faouzi Skali. I did not know how to react. I was happy, of course, for proof that my letter had reached the correct destination. But who was Fabrice, and what was the reason for this intermediary?

When I met Fabrice the next day at a pizzeria in Montparnasse where we had agreed to rendezvous, to me he looked like the most ordinary kind of white man in his late thirties, whose appearance shouted middle management. After several seconds, he introduced himself more fully than he had over the phone the night before. His Muslim first name was Idrss, and he was *moqaddem* (head) of the Parisian branch of the tariqa to which Faouzi Skali belonged. The exact name of this brotherhood was tariqa al Qadiriya Butchichiya, and Sidi Hamza al Qadiri al Butchichi, fourteenth descendent of the famous *mawlay* Abd al Qadir al Jilani, who lived in Morocco, had been its spiritual teacher since 1972. He then asked me a series of questions, and by way of response, I recounted my entire life story.

He seemed satisfied at the end of my tale and told me, in turn, of his own journey, which was completely different but just as atypical. The child of a good family who grew up in the sixteenth arrondissement of Paris, he had pursued his higher studies with a particular interest in spirituality; the twists and turns of his personal quest had even taken him through Freemasonry before discovering the Sufi path and embracing Islam. Over dessert, he suggested that I attend one of their meetings—only if I wanted to, he added. He must have been fully aware that this last precaution was purely rhetorical and that I had been dreaming of nothing else for a long time.

In the metro, I smiled and said hello to everyone whose gaze crossed mine, and intoxicated with intense happiness, I recollected the poem by the great Rumi:

> *You have reached the dungeons of the heart: now stop*
> *   here.*
> *Since you have seen this moon, now stop here.*
> *You have dragged your rags*
> *In all directions out of ignorance: now stop here.*
> *A life has flowed past, and by the grace of this moon*
> *You have heard so much talk about it: now stop here.*
> *Gaze at this beauty, for it is his vision*
> *That makes you visible or invisible: now stop here.*
> *The milk that runs in your breast is the same milk you*
> *   drank from the breast: now stop here.*

A smiling fifty-year-old black man opened the door, greeted me, and told me where to find the bathroom to perform my ablutions. I had heard a low murmur since entering the apartment. After I had taken off my shoes, the man opened a glass door in front me, and the murmur abruptly transformed into clear Arabic: *La ilaha illa"llah,* "There is no God but Allah." A dozen people of all ages and colors, seated in a circle, were loudly repeating this declaration of the Muslim faith.

My limbs shivered, and my heart began beating faster. A prophetic hadith basically says that when a group of people gather to invoke God, the angels surround them with their wings from the earth to the heavens. I knew these traditional words, but in the meetings I had participated in, despite the reading of the Qur'an and the invocation of God, never in my whole life had I felt what I was experiencing when taking a place in this circle. This was a *true* circle. I had a personal conviction that there were more people in the room than appeared to be there. I had never tasted such intoxication.

Six months later, I was an official member of the al Qadiriya Butchichiya Brotherhood, and I found myself flying to Morocco again. Naouale had asked me one evening—out of curiosity as she is Moroccan—if I knew in what city this teacher Sidi Hamza, whose disciple I had become without ever meeting him in person, lived. I had no idea and therefore had to find the information for myself before giving her an answer: The spiritual leader of the brotherhood lived at the head zawiya in a small village named Madagh in the Oujda region of eastern Morocco, close to the Algerian border.

This answer took Naouale aback: her own family came from this village, which was so tiny that it did not appear on any map! I viewed this as a positive sign, and I later learned that Sidi Hamza was in the habit of repeating: "We often think that it is we who are going toward the Way, but in reality it is the Way that is coming to us!" It was I who took the plane, but in reality it was he who was coming toward me, without my knowing.

In the jargon of the mosques that I frequented, we often had the opportunity to say that so-and-so had *nour,* meaning his face was luminous; but this was often merely a metaphor for saying that he looked

well! When in the simple room where Sidi Hamza welcomed me and
I saw this man dressed in white with an equally immaculate white
beard—even his skin seemed to be the same milky color—I understood
for the first time what this expression really meant. Sidi Hamza's gaze
met mine, and in a fraction of a second I was transported by this vision
of an ocean of love. His extraordinary smile made him even more beautiful, and I would hardly have been able to guess his age if I did not
already know that he was eighty years old. His voice was both firm and
gentle, and his glasses were powerless to veil his clear, sparkling, and
incredibly young gaze.

He bid us all welcome in Arabic. A person sitting near him acted
as his translator. The room was filled to bursting. I took a moment to
look at the group assembled around me: blacks, whites, Arabs, and even
Asians, young and old alike commingled together. The Qur'an basically
says that the different cultures are so many kinds of wealth that make
it possible for individuals to meet each other. But I had not often witnessed this, except at the home of Faouzi Skali.

Sidi Hamza began to speak:

"In the time of the Prophet (PSL)," he told us, "the relationship
existing between the Companions, the fraternity that prevailed, the way
they shared everything, the preference they showed others over themselves, and their spirit of sacrifice all had its origin in Love. In the same
way, men of God bear the fountain of this Love in their hearts. The one
who drinks from it can never forget it. He has obtained a beverage after
which no thirst is possible. Hearts attuned, minds are in affinity. This
is the Kingdom of God!"

Every year on the occasion of the Laylat al-Qâdr (the Night of Fate),
more than twenty thousand disciples of every nationality from all over
the entire world (black Africa, North Africa, Europe, the United States,
Asia, the Middle East) made their way to the zawiya of Madagh. The
entire palette of humanity was represented there on this occasion. It
was magnificent. The days that followed at the zawiya were spent in
prayer, invocations, and bursts of laughter. I felt light as a feather, as if

the ballast of my self had been jettisoned. I had the impression of being able to see after being blind. I now tasted Islam as if I were biting into a delicious fruit.

Despite all the diplomatic wealth we were able to deploy toward BMG, the album never managed to take off, which led me to redefine my position concerning rap. Without renouncing anything of my history in this musical genre, I felt free to put my commitment to it into perspective. I was no longer a rapper; I was first and foremost Abd al Malik. I no longer wanted my activities to be a mask that hid me from myself—which did not mean abandoning them, it meant simply putting them back in their proper place.

Naouale was preparing to release her first album, and things were working out well for her. I meanwhile took advantage of my technical unemployment to spend time with my son and lead an intense spiritual life that kept taking me back and forth from Paris to the remote village where my spiritual teacher lived. However, even when I was in the deepest reaches of Morocco, I could not prevent myself from thinking about music, and no doubt my constant trips were a way to flee. Finally, because I was unable to drive rap out of my mind, I was forced to admit that it meant more to me than I had thought.

Some time earlier, during the course of a journey at the time of the last week of Ramadan, I had gotten to know Fabien—his Muslim first name was Badr. He was a disciple of the same brotherhood as me whose path had already crossed mine at dhikr sessions in southern France. This twenty-eight-year-old white, a rather handsome boy, had followed a fairly unique path. Born in a relatively well-off environment, his parents were professors, and he practiced kinesitherapy and osteopathy. He had also felt a pathological hatred for blacks and Arabs during his adolescence as a result of being assaulted. However, his spiritual path had led him to embrace Islam, and at present he had been living close to the sheik for almost a year. Everything opposed us: our skin color, our social origins, our professional lives. . . . The only thing that brought us together was our quest for the essential. During the Night of Fate, after a veritable communion of souls, we had talked together as if we had always known one another, and with Aïssa, who was also there—he had recently entered the Path—we decided to give new enthusiasm to our music.

It was my love of writing that led to my involvement with rap, and I had come to Islam because my hero of that time, the Brooklyn rapper Big Daddy Kane, claimed to be Muslim. No record had made as deep an impression on me as his first album, released in 1988, *Long Live the Kane,* which combined the harshness of the ghetto, poetry, subversion, showing off, and spirituality. This monument had forced all rappers to question their own approach. In 1994, when our first record, *Trop beau pour être vrai* [Too Handsome to Be True] was released, we were a hundred leagues from imagining that rap was already dead.

Yet the same year, this was what the New York rapper Nas proclaimed in his brilliant first album: "Somehow the rap game reminds me of the crack game." In other words, the business of rap had grown similar to the marketing of hard drugs: people were content to furnish the public the dope it demanded, and if possible, to cut it as much as possible. French rap had already mutated into a veritable mass industry, despite its persistent image of a subculture saved by its antiestablishment appearance. I remained convinced, though, that no rapper was as true and pure as us while so many puppets were swarming all over. We alone had a legitimate right to speak of the ghetto and force the whole of France to look at the projects in a new light. All we needed was to package it with an authenticity guaranteed to seduce the largest possible public. And Big Daddy Kane was the perfect package.

When *La racaille sort un disque* came out two years later, I expected to be acclaimed everywhere. I could already see the journalists striving to discover us and question us on the apparent and hidden themes in our music, which would permit me to sport the ironic smile of someone who intends to prove his infinite profundity behind his high tops and cap. I did not want to see that I had it wrong and I did not understand the gaze—blended with admiration and rejection—that our peers turned on us, and even less that they were seeing a touch of Parisian bias in us. Despite the celebrity that the commercial success of the album had brought us, failure was already in the cards: rap was too deeply eaten away by the cancer of stupidity, violence, one-upmanship, and lies.

As a marginal group offering a marginal music, moreover one from a low-income housing project in Strasbourg, we should have been happy with getting good reviews from the critics and with being in Paris to talk about our album. This frustrating pattern repeated itself for the next two albums: what we said was endorsed by the industry but did not speak to anyone. I had to wait until that Night of Fate to grasp that up to the present we had always been seeking to prove that we were the purest and the most profound—without ever being content with how we *were*. It was this claim of authenticity that was perverting our approach, despite all the affectation of our words. I then decided to commit myself to rap as an entirely separate art, and to live my texts rather than put them on stage. In music as in life, I decided not to retranscribe the mentality of the relevance of the moment, but to simply translate the language of the heart. This was the approach I decided to adopt for my first solo album.

FIVE

ON THE PATH TO THE OTHER

Time was I would criticize my neighbor
If his religion was not the same as mine
But now my heart welcomes every form
It is a prairie for the gazelles and
A cloister for monks
A temple for idols and
A Kaaba for the pilgrim
The Tables of the Torah and the Book of the Qur'an
I follow the religion of Love and whatever
Direction taken by Love's camel, that is my religion and
my faith.

FROM THE SONG "ODE TO LOVE"

During an evening of spiritual drunkenness at the zawiya in Morocco, Fabien and I wrote an "Ode to Love," which I decided to preface with these verses of Ibn Arabi and put to music. The ocean of universal love professed by the man who is called "the greatest of teachers" penetrated every pore of my being. I wished to make it mine, speak it, transmit it, and share it.

On my return to Paris, I stumbled upon a cultural show on the radio in which a certain Émile Shoufani, an Israeli Arab priest, was mounting an appeal for compassion and suggesting to Jews and Muslims that they travel and gather together at Auschwitz. I shared the emotions this stirred in me with Naouale, who also expressed her admiration for this message. According to her, all those who wanted peace should grab this extended hand in order to get out of the current confusion and show up, not as Hebrew or Arab, Jew or Muslim, but as simply a man. Someone was stepping forward to lay the first stone of reconciliation, not only of the Israelis and the Palestinians, not only of the Jews and Arabs of France, but also of man with himself.

It was my imperative duty to agree to take part in this journey when my friend Rachid Benzine invited me a short time later. What more concrete proof of love could there be than sharing the pain of one's brother while standing at his side, all the more reason when his Jewish identity and my Islamic faith could distance us from each other a priori, taking into account the surrounding tension? To share someone else's suffering is to make oneself available for rejoicing together one day, for building a new world together—in short to live!

On arriving at the seminar that would prepare us for this trip—three days with survivors, historians, and the incredibly luminous Father Émile—I was delighted to recognize many friends whose faces had marked my spiritual journey, especially the Bordeaux imam Tariq Oubrou, who was present at the side of the young Muslims of France. Even Faouzi Skali and Cheikh Bentounes, who we had met in Strasbourg, were with us spiritually; they appeared on the list of supporters who had responded to the appeal made by the priest of Nazareth! I found there the most significant figures of my spiritual path, those who had permitted me to rise above my despair when I was in a total crisis about Islam such as I had then practiced it. But I found them at the crossroads, having personally made the decision to undertake this itinerary, which I realized was natural to those who lived Islam as a path of openness and love. Many other Muslims involved in the community were also mingling with our Jewish brothers, and the incredible promise that was so rich in this image gave me great joy.

The plane landed two hours late in a sun-drenched Krakow that irresistibly reminded me of Strasbourg. When climbing into one of the twelve tour buses—there were five hundred of us, coming from Israel, France, and Belgium—I was reminded of the day that I, for the first time, had traveled on the bus with Majid to the mosque. I recalled the questioning silence of the Lubavitch Jew we had asked directions from when lost. Yes, it is true, I had really asked a Jew how to get to the mosque!

Until this time, the Jews had been a reality and a culture too far removed for me to have taken much interest in them, and I had hardly known any personally except those I had met in the music world, with whom I got along just fine. I had happened now and then to overhear more or less anti-Semitic remarks in certain mosques, but I paid no more attention to them than I would to any other manifestations of human stupidity, such as the anti-Turk, anti-Asian, or antiblack remarks that I heard on a daily basis. I had had the opportunity of reading Primo Levi, but oddly enough, I had never made the connection between the absolute horror of the Shoah and the verbal anti-Semitism I had observed in my former companions. Over the course of the seminar in Paris, however, I realized that the annihilation of a people originates in words and actions that appear completely banal and that are, in fact, transporting a deadly ideology.

The spiritual labor that I had undertaken under Sidi Hamza henceforth made it impossible for me to rationalize in terms of black, Arab, or Jew, for all *I* saw were human beings. Our teacher had told us that hidden within each human being is the *sirr,* the "spiritual secret," and for this reason every human being is precious. The Shoah, a genocide that was made even more terrible by its industrial scope and the modernity of its death factories, may only have touched a definite fraction of humanity directly, but it concerned the entire human race—and equally.

After visiting the remnants of the ghetto, during which an Israeli delegation placed a bouquet at the foot of the last remaining portion of its enceinte wall, we were taken to visit the famous Schindler factory. There, we met up with a Palestinian delegation with whom Majid (now back from Syria for good), Mohammed (who had not hesitated a moment when this trip was announced), and I exchanged a warm *"Salaam oua likoum."* Majid conversed with the members of this delegation for several minutes in very literate Arabic, which he had mastered to perfection. I listened without understanding a word, grasping only that their presence on these premises was motivated solely by their insatiable desire for peace.

We then entered a large synagogue that the Nazis had used for a stable and that has been magnificently renovated. This was an unprecedented step for me, setting foot in a synagogue, duly covered by a yarmulke. I felt the same serenity I encountered when entering a mosque. The interior architecture was surprisingly reminiscent of one, while also bringing to mind a cathedral, or rather a Protestant church. Noticing a glassed recess on the back wall, I asked Nathan and Gabriel, two young men with whom we had become friends on the plane, what its meaning was. My surprise was complete when they explained that this recess indicated the direction of Jerusalem, in the East, just as in a mosque a similar recess indicated the direction of Mecca! During the visit to the Jewish cemetery, I continued to appreciate the symbolic correspondences of our two religions. After returning to the hotel, I almost wept for joy when recalling the image of a priest, an imam, and a rabbi holding hands in a synagogue and appealing for peace in one voice at the memorial. . . .

After waking at dawn, taking just enough time to pray and eat breakfast, we climbed aboard a bus that took us one hour outside of Krakow to Birkenau, the extermination camp that was part of the Auschwitz complex. On the bus trip, I was blinded by a flash of conscience when a woman full of energy pointed out the place where she had worked as a slave. An aura radiated from her that was incredibly vital and gentle. One felt, from the serenity she exhibited when mentioning these terrible events, that she had turned a page, that she had "chosen life," as it is said in the Torah, that she was not trapped in the past, but enriched the present with her memories.

The testimony of Schlomo Venezia, another survivor, found the same echo in me, although their experiences were different. He had been a member of the *Sonderkommandos,* groups of Jews obliged under penalty of instant death "to oversee" the running of the gas chambers. These witnesses and others were all invested with words intended to make our memory a rampart against the stupidity and horror that are engendered by forgetfulness. They spoke to us, Muslims and Arabs, with wisdom and fraternity, and without the slightest trace of judgment, distance, or mistrust.

Their injured memory was a living memory, completely oriented toward being shared, and it irresistibly reminded me of the primary meaning of the dhikr that we practiced in the brotherhood. The dhikr, which is the recollection of the name of God, souvenir and remembrance, can be found in the Hebrew root "zkr" that appears so often in the Torah. By remembering together absolute inhumanity, we were also remembering together the urgency of Love. And this shared memory was a sign of hope, for as the saying puts it: "If we remember Love, Love will remember us."

Six months later, the winter darkness swallowing the sky had not yet managed to stifle the noise of the projects when my taxi let me out at the entrance to Neuhof as I had requested. Only the wan light of the streetlamps made it possible to make out the vertical expanse of the towers, now eaten by the night. As I was paying my fare, the taxi driver made his apologies for not driving me farther: "You know, if we refuse to take customers into Neuhof, it is not really because we are scared, but at times the kids become hyper after night falls, and they pelt our cars with a flood of stones. . . . You understand, personally I don't have anything against Arabs, or blacks—incidentally my sister-in-law is from Guadeloupe—but it's my car—you understand, it's how I earn my living. . . ."

"Of course, I understand," I had answered him with a sincere smile before plunging into this neighborhood I knew by heart. Here, this small crossing was where I had hunted for customers when I was a dealer; there were the telephone booths where I had gone through countless phone cards talking with Naouale; at this stop, I caught the bus 14 to go "to work. . . ." The mosque had become a simple annex since the faithful had been able to acquire a part of a Protestant church. My entire life filed past me in several hundred yards. . . .

Several weeks earlier, a young woman I had met on my trip to Auschwitz had invited me to perform a rap piece at a meeting against communitarianism* organized by the Union of French Jewish Students. I found it quite amusing to tell myself that I would be performing one of the titles of my new album for the first time before a Jewish audience, and the highly symbolic value of this event delighted me.

But this was not the sole reason for my return to Strasbourg. Bilal had been maintaining an e-mail correspondence with our father for several years, and this latter had confirmed his arrival for today! It had been planned for me to pick him up at Roissy and drive him to Neuhof, where his ex-wife—my mother—and his other children still lived. Unfortunately, the French authorities had demanded additional paperwork from him before giving him a visa, which delayed his arrival by a month. We were disappointed, of course, but after fifteen years of separation, this month would seem like only a day to us. There was no hatred or bitterness in any of us, and our gaze remained fixed on the horizon of our reunion.

When I passed before the minimarket that had been the theater for my enflamed preaching, I realized that all the faces I spotted beneath Lacoste visors were unknown to me—each and every one. Yet, before I had been on familiar terms with every inhabitant of the quarter. This

---

*[This refers to the movement that appeared in the mid '90s—demanding special rights for cultural, racial, or religious minorities—which protested, for one thing, the law that forbade Muslim schoolgirls to wear head scarves; this movement generated a great controversy in France. —*Trans.*]

realization let me fully feel the weight of my twenty-eight years on my shoulders. There were no longer but a handful of us veterans, the survivors of a generation that madness, death, or prison had decimated. As I drew near my building, I noticed a police wagon and an unmarked car, a Safrane whose typical maneuvers indicated its driver was an agent of the BAC. The notorious presence of dealers on this block made me initially think it was a raid for dope or shit, but I knew at the same time that it was too late in the day for them to have been able to obtain a valid search warrant—to borrow official police jargon.

Suddenly, I spotted my little brother Stéphane leaving the apartment, and the policemen moving into action once he closed the door behind him. What had he done now? What had happened to him? Without wasting any more time trying to figure out an answer, having only my mother's face in mind, I started running to cross the final hundred yards separating me from the building.

EPILOGUE

As a rapper and as an artist, I continue to ask questions of, or rather to probe more deeply into, the questions that life has given and continues to give me. The answers I come up with inform both my art and my life. I deeply believe that at this crucial time of globalization, terrorism, and major environmental problems, music—and art in general—can no longer be regarded as simple amusements but should be seen as fundamental energizers, as a means for beginning to concretely resolve the problems of this world. In many respects, our days are numbered and reversing these problems becomes a little more impossible with every passing second. There is thus a sense of urgency on this path to reorient art and culture, as they are such powerful vehicles; they alone are capable of touching the whole individual on the deepest, most fundamental, level.

Every artist—or anyone who claims to be one—should seriously take action here or, in my opinion, they are unworthy of the title. Revitalizing art and culture is the purpose of my music. And undoubtedly because of my personal life history, it also seeks to be a tool for radically changing the truncated view of Islam that has predominated since September 11, 2001. I am a Muslim, the disciple of a great spiritual teacher, and with my words I seek to shake humanity from its customary lethargy—a humanity that every day appears to be losing a little more of what gives its life a foundation. So while we tell ourselves that there is a pressing urgency, my approach is first and foremost an invitation, an invitation to enter a new era without any hang-ups: a new era characterized by understanding, acceptance, and responsibility.

Shortly after the publication of this book in France, I was able to see the extent to which it deeply affected the way people lived. It allowed individuals from all socio-cultural milieus, colors, and religious denominations—who all too often had been prisoners of their fears—to connect with another dimension of themselves and to reconnect with their heart. Globalization is not a plague but a gift, provided that it permits humanity to raise itself into a modernity capable of feeding on this legacy that we call spiritual traditions, this universal light that I call God.

LYRIC EXTRACTS FROM THE ALBUM
LE FACE À FACE DES COEURS
[HEARTS FACE TO FACE]

Atmosphériques/Universal, 2004

QUE DIEU BÉNISSE LA FRANCE

J'aime cette terre qui m'a faire
Faut l'dire pas juste contester
S'diviser l'passé l'temps est à l'unité
Mais faut bien que j'avoue gamin j'ai voulu changer de
*   tête*
Et bien sûr qu'c'est triste d'exclure un enfant d'une fête
Trop longtemps j'ai pris sur moi la rancoeur devient
*   voile*
Aprés on s'dit normal moi aussi j'dois leur faire mal
C'est une sorte de parodie on s'dit y a moi et puis y a
*   l'autre*
On s'enferme dans un role et lautre devient d'trop,
*   faux?*

Et je suppose qu'on s'éloigne plus de soi-même

*Le non-amour une tragédie j'suis l'premier à demander
de l'aide*

*Je voudrais être sage comme Heraclite, qu'autour ça
sente plus la poudre*

*On a l'même sang qui coule rouge, qu'importe l'idée,
l'principe*

*Trouve une autre peau éthique, plus positive frère
n'oublie pas l'temps presse*

Avant que n'arrive le terme faut bien qu'on s'unisse

Au lieu qu'on s'déchire qu'on s' fasse des batailles

*Parce que si déjà on s'sourit ça veut dire qui reste de
l'espoir*

Si déjà on s'sourit ça veut dire qu'on peut y croire

Si déjà on s'sourit ça veut dire qu'il ya du savoir

La fin du monde s'est passé a l'interieue de moi

*Après l'apocalypse c'est fou c'est maintenant que je suis
moi*

*C'est l'Amour qu'j'ai pour race plus une couleur comme
insigne*

Regarde comme je plane sans même fumer de shit

Regarde comme je brave toutes sortes de stereotypes

*J'suis citoyen d'un univers où chacun est son pire
ennemi*

Si je reussis à vaincre mon proper ego

T'auras devant toi l'vrai moi et plus seulement l' faux

*Si t'as des ennemis c'est pas vraiment eux qu'il faut
craindre des assauts*

Et j'suis sorti du coma pour restriendre mes defauts, oh!

La même étoile au-dessus d'nos têtes à tous scintilla

*Ma mere m'a toujours dit que tous le même rêve on
poursuit*

Mais tu sais c'est pas la vice qui m'instruit

La quête de l'Amour je poursuis je suis l'esclave de
    l'Amour
Parce que c'est la sève, la substance de cette vie
On n'est qu'acteurs "coupez!" et notre film est fini
Le bien domine c'est juste à toi de choisir
Le don de la vie precieux dommage qu'in n'en fasse pas
    notre profit
Le bien une offrande, des fruits sur l'autel de cette vie
Tu sens bien qu'ici y a une presence l'Amour doit être la
    norme
J'm'envole décolle là où ya plus d'conflit
Et je m'nourris du nectar qu'sécrète cette vie
Y a plus d'problème ris, profitons d'la vie, elle n'a pas
    de prix
Soyons tous ensemble amis
Tu sais j'aime c'pays le ressens-tu dans ce que je dis Ami
    soyons tous ensemble en harmonie que l'on donne ou
Qu'on reçoive que l'on reste ami
Pour toi et moi prie que Dieu bénisse la France c'est un
    si beau pays

Derrière les apparences, n'y a-t-il pas un même coeur
    qui bat?
Sur ce champ infini de la mémoire, n'y a-t-il que des
    épouvantails?
L'enfant s'est-il véritablement dissous, dans ce visage
    d'adulte crispé?
Le salut est-il possible hors de la tendresse, de la
    compassion et de l'Amour?
Étais-tu donc absent? L'argent, l'alcool et la violence,
    c'est mon proper vide que tu tentais de remplir
Étais-tu donc sourd? Mes attitudes et mes chansons c'est
    à l'aide qu'il fallait lire

*Étais-tu donc aveugle? Nos parents ont sacrifié pour
    cette demeure*
Comment as-tu pu me demander de partir
*Étais-tu donc muet? Lorsque comme un seul homme,
    nous nous sommes levés*
C'est merci qu'il fallait dire
*Derrière les apparences je me suis éteint à mon
    extinction*
*Sur le champ infini de la mémoire, l'Amour seul a pu
    éclore*
*L'enfant seul peut défaire les chaînes et sortir de la
    caverne somber du monde des ombres, de l'existence*
Hors de l'Amour, il n'y a point de Salut
*Le sage est devenu, en appliquant sur ses yeux cette
    argile mouillé par les larmes*
Que Dieu bénisse la terre qui nous a redone la vue

Translation:

ALLAH BLESS FRANCE

I love this land that formed me
Gotta say so not just protest
Divided in the past, time's now come for unity
But I really gotta confess that as a kid I really wanted
    to change my head
And you know there's nothing sadder than excluding a
    child from a party
For too long I took upon myself resentment turned
    into a veil
After someone claims to be normal I too should hurt
    them
It is a kind of parody that someone tells me then tells
    the other

A person imprisons himself in a role and the other
    becomes too much, no?
And I suppose this takes one even farther from oneself
Nonlove is a tragedy I am the first to ask for help
I want to be wise as Heraclitus, because it smells more
    like gunpowder everywhere
We have the same blood that runs red, no matter what
    idea or principle
Find another ethical more positive skin brother don't
    forget that time is pressing
Before the end comes we really need to be united
Otherwise people will be tearing each other to pieces,
    they will be fighting each Other
Because if someone is already smiling it implies that
    hope remains
If someone is already smiling it implies it is still
    possible to believe
If someone is already smiling it implies that there is
    knowledge
The end of the world took place inside me
After the apocalypse it's crazy it's now that I am me
It's Love that I have for race no longer a color like an
    insignia
Look how high I soar without even smoking any shit
Look how I brave all kinds of stereotypes
I am the citizen of a world where everyone is his own
    worst enemy
If I succeed in vanquishing my own ego
You'll have the real me before you and not just the
    false anymore
If you have enemies it is not really them you should be
    scared of attacking you
And I emerged from my coma to limit my flaws, oh!

The same star above our heads has sparkled for all

My mother always told me that everyone is pursuing
   the same dream

But you know that it is not vice that teaches me

The quest of Love I am pursuing I am the slave of
   Love

Because it is the sap and substance of this life

We are only actors "cut!" and our film is over

Good prevails it is up to you to choose

The precious gift of life too bad no one turns it to our
   advantage

Good is an offering, fruits on the altar of this life

You clearly feel that there is a presence Love should be
   the standard

I take off flying wherever conflict has vanished

And I feed on the nectar secreted by this life

There is no more problem, laugh, let's profit from this
   life, it is priceless

Let's all be friends together

Ya know I love this country d'ya feel it in what I say,
   Friend?

Let's all be in harmony together whether we are giving
   or receiving let's remain friends

For you and me I pray that God bless France; it's such
   a fine country

Isn't it the same heart beating behind appearances?

Are there nothing but scarecrows on memory's infinite
   field?

Is the child truly dissolved within this stressed-out
   adult face?

Is salvation possible outside of tenderness, compassion,
   and Love?

So were you away? Money, alcohol, and violence, it was
my own emptiness you were attempting to fill

So were you deaf? My attitudes and songs are the help
that needs to be read

So were you blind? Our parents sacrificed so much for
this home

How can you ask me to leave

Were you mute then? When we rose up as one man?

You need to give thanks

Behind appearances I was impervious to my own
extinction

Love alone could hatch on this infinite field of
memory,

The child alone can undo the chains and emerge from
the dark cavern of shadows, of life

Outside of Love there is no salvation

The sage has become one by placing this clay
moistened with tears over his eyes

May God bless the land that has restored our sight.

LETTRE À MON PÈRE

Très cher papa, j'aurais voulu partager avec toi cette
*   lettre le prouve*
Prends pour preuve mon coeur que je t'ouvre
Très cher papa, j'aurais aimé que ma plume soit plus
*   légère l'absence d'un trop-plein de mots aurait dit*
*   combien je t'aime*
Très cher papa, lis cette letter selon ce qu'elle vaut
*   l'ultime propos je t'aime dans chacun de mes mots*
Très cher papa, une famille c'est tellement beau je parle
*   comme la perle qui perle sur ton visage*
Tu vois la douleur de maman elle fut grande papa
Blessé par l'absence pourquoi t'es pas là papa
Maintenant que he suis pèreà mon tour à mon fils je
*   donne de l'amour*
Sur le temps ineluctable nul n'a le pouvoir du retour
*   virgule*
Rien de bon peut être base sur la haine
Et dans le cas present les regrets n'entraînent que la
*   peine virgule*
Ton fils qui t'aime. P.S. t'embrasse avec tendress
Je t'aime. . . .

Refrain
Malgré l'absence de mon père j'ai quand même grandi
Y a pas de chance ni de malchance c'est juste la vie
Et si j'ai écrit cette lettre c'est pour te le dire
Ainsi va la vie l'amour pas la haine pour reconstruire

Très cher papa, je vais te parler avec mon coeur et sans
*   haine t'inquiète pas même pas une arrière pensée*
Juste un bilan depuis ton depart en 83

Laissant trois petits avec leur mere bref
Papa je t'aime tu sais mais là t'as deconné
Fallait pas partir fallait pas quitter le navire
À un certain niveau papa tu sais on part pas
Une famille encore plus belle, une famille encore plus
     forte
Le souhait de toi et maman à vingt ans
Mais que faire face à la volunté supreme
La marionette est soumise au Marionnettiste
Et c'est sûr papa je te pardonne

Refrain

Je peux offrir mon âme au pillage désormais moi
J'ai trouvé l'Amour c'est pour ça que je t'écris papa
Que m'importe les gains, les pertes, l'Amour est mon
     trône
Je suis un mari, un fils, un père, l'Amour ma couronne
Y a plus de drame n'est-ce pas singulier l'Amour ma
     flamme
Je n'ai plus de prétexte j'ôte les habits de mon âme,
     j'ôte les facéties de mon ego et ma haine part en
     lambeaux
Si bien qu'a present je vois clair l'Amour tomba ma
     bandeau
Je parle à la bêtise de l'air sort de nos têtes
Éloigne-toi de nous, rétracte tes griffes qui servent
A perdre nos âmes, je t'écris ça pa'
Sache que ton fils raisonne
L'Amour est la seule chose qu'il te porte

Refrain

Translation:

LETTER TO MY FATHER

Dear papa, I wanted to share with you this letter
    proves it
Take as proof the heart that I am opening to you
Dear papa, I would rather my pen was lighter, the
    absence of an overflow of words would have told
    you how much I love you
Dear papa, read this letter based on the worth of its
    last sentence, I love you in every word
Dear papa, a family is so beautiful I am talking like
    the pearl that beads on your forehead
You see mama's pain was so great, papa
Wounded by your absence, why aren't you here papa?
Now that I am a father to my son I give love in turn
No one has the power over inevitable time to return
    comma
Nothing good can be founded on hate
And in the present case regrets bring nothing but pain
    comma
Your son who loves you. P.S. with a tender hug
I love you. . . .

Refrain
Despite the absence of my father I still grew up
It is not good luck or bad luck it's just life
And if I wrote this letter it is to tell you that
That's how in life it is love not hate that rebuilds

Dear papa, I am going to speak to you from the heart
    and without hatred don't worry about any ulterior
    motive

Just a balance sheet since you left in '83
Leaving three little kids with their mother in short
Papa, I love you, but you screwed up that time
Shouldn't be leaving shouldn't be abandoning ship
On a certain level papa you know no one leaves
A family that is even more beautiful a family that is
    even stronger
The desire of you and mama when you were twenty
But confronted by the supreme will
The marionette submits to the puppeteer
And sure thing papa I forgive you

Refrain

I can offer my soul to be pillaged henceforth
I've found Love and that is why I'm writing you papa
What do gains and losses matter to me? Love is my
    throne
I am a husband, a son, a father, Love my crown
There is no more drama isn't my flame of Love so
    singular?
I have no more pretexts I have taken off the habits of
    my soul, I remove the pranks of my ego and my
    hatred breaks into shreds
So much that at present I clearly see Love has knocked
    off my blindfold
I speak to the stupidity of the air emerging from our
    heads
Go away from me, pull in your claws that serve
To lose our souls, I write you this pa
Know that your son is reasonable
Love is the only thing he bears for you

Refrain

TRACES DES LUMIÈRE

Yeah ma voix se baisse parce que mon coeur se tait je le
*   sais*
Le bruit n'est que silence statique est la cadence je
*   tombe*
Je sais pas si vous le sentez vous piéger comme un
*   animal je sais plus à me cramponner*
Je viens d'où? Où est-ce que je vais? Qu'est-ce que j'en
*   sais ces questions plus je me les poses plus je souffre*
Mes amis rient de moi, mais j'ai honte de parler de ma
*   différence*
S'ils me quittent l'absence se muera en souffrance plus
*   grande encore que celle qui me vide*
Qu'est-ce que j'ai ou bien qu'est-ce que j'ai pas?!
Qui je suis ou bien qui je suis pas?!
Je m'enfonce chaque jour un peu plus dans ce trou qui se
*   prend pour moi*
Même cette mélancholie qu'on disait cool me peine
Je pourrais presque dire combien y a d'étoiles dans le
*   ciel*
En termes spirituals la quête en moi y a trop de
*   mystères*

Refrain
Y a Kalifan

Tout me préjuge j'ai peur d'ennuyer donc he reste seul
Mais comme je sais pas vraiment ce que je recherche je
*   feins le fun*
Spleen grave et la donne rien ne me sourit
C'est comme si rien n'avait de sens qu'est-ce qui
*   changerait ma vie*

J'ai passé trop de nuits à pleurer, quand la jour va se lever?

Comme si quelque chose en fait m'était occulté

Ce à quoi je m'accroche en sorte ne sont que des specters

Je respecte mais ma quête va au-délà

Je suis si jeune pourquoi je me prends la tête comme ça

Quand tu penses que la plupart vit dans l'insouciance

Je suis dos au mur feignant de jouer mon proper role

Désaxé par rapport au pôle

J'ai peur de devinir fou par manque de l'amour

La conscience n-t-elle pas fait sauter mon tour

Ma vie c'est juste une vêtement pour faire comme et surtout pas autrement

Refrain

En seize measures le récit d'une vie passée la mienne

Vous m'avez tous vu rigoler de bonne humeur

Vous avez cru voir se dégager de moi le bonheur

Ce n'est pas le reflet qu'ol y avait dans le coeur

Ce que je voulais moi c'était la paix intérieur

La vraie, infinie, celle qui est dans le coeur

J'ai cru la trouver en compagnie des femmes

En buvant de l'alcool et an ayant beaucoup d'argent

C'est pas la paix que j'ai eue moi c'est le malaise

Un truc malsaine dans un coeur vide

Quand le coeur est malade le corps souffre

Résultat j'étais mal j'avais pas la cause

Normal je buvais à la mauvaise source

La source de la paix intérieur est une

Y boire donne la vie au coeur et au corps

J'ai vécu vivant avex un coeur mort

Refrain

Translation:

TRACES OF LIGHT

Yeah, my voice lowers because my heart has stopped
    speaking I know
Noise is only silence the cadence is static I fall
I don't know if you feel it traps you like an animal I no
    longer know what to cling to
Where am I coming from? Where am I going?
    Whatever I know these questions the more I ask
    them the more I suffer
My friends laugh at me, and I'm ashamed to talk of my
    difference
If they leave me the absence will transform into an
    even greater suffering than the one emptying me
What do I have or else what don't I have?!
Who am I or else who am I not?!
Every day I bury myself a little deeper in this hole that
    thinks it's me
Even this melancholy people call cool hurts me
I could almost say how many stars there are in the sky
In spiritual terms there are too many mysteries in the
    quest into myself

Refrain
Kafilan is there

Everyone prejudges me I am scared of being boring so I
    stay alone
But because I am not really what I am looking for I
    pretend to be having fun
Serious spleen and the cards dealt nothing smiles on
    me

It's like nothing had any meaning that would change
    my life
I have spent too many nights weeping, when will the
    sun rise?
It's like something was being hid from me
The things I try to hang on to are nothing but
    specters
I have respect but my quest goes beyond
I am so young that I take the lead like this
When you think that most people live not caring
My back is to the wall pretending to play my own role
Unhinged by comparison to the pole
I am scared of going mad for lack of love
Awareness has not exploded my tower
My life is only a piece of clothing for doing like this
    and especially not otherwise

Refrain

In sixteen measures the tale of a past life my
    own
You have all seen me in a good mood kidding
You think you saw happiness getting free of me
This is not the reflection that was in my heart
What I really wanted was inner peace
The true and infinite one that is in the heart
I thought I found it in the company of women
In drinking alcohol and having lots of money
It is not peace I had but uneasiness
An unhealthy gimmick in an empty heart
When the heart is sick the body suffers
Result I was sick but did not know the cause
Normal I drank from the bad spring

The spring of inner peace is one
Where drinking gives life to heart and body
I have experienced living with a dead heart

Refrain

NOIR & BLANC

Mesdames, mesdemoiselles, et messieurs, musique!

Intro
Oh Non, Non, Non, Non, Oh, Oh Oh Oh Oh Oh
Le Noir allume les lumières la nuit
Le Blanc éteint le sombre de nos tristes nuits
Que te dire sinon faut qu'on soit Ami
Noir & Blanc c'est la même je te l'ai déjà dit

Laisse moi te dire hier moi j'étais ce Blanc, sang rouge
    si différent
Je vivais si loin de l'autre des que j'ai vécu cette scène
Un couteau sale petit-bourgeois donne-moi tout ce que
    tu as sur toi
La peur, la rage m'ont cloisonné dans la haine (men)
Sème comme cette graine, entraîne le malheur
Tant de vicissitude égrenée par le rancoeur
Et la haine se multiplie d'elle je suis prisonnier
De part et d'autre voyons tout cela n'entraîne que la
    peine
Tout cela est commun comme phénomène
Je veux dire c'est juste un épiphénomène
L'addition de ce genre d'événement mène toujours vers
La soustraction des nobles sentiments d'hier
Sale "bip" espèce de gros "bip," allez-vous faire "bip"
Retournez d'où vous êtes venus si vous êtes déçus
Ce hier, c'est le hier de tant de gens, au sang rouge si
    différent

Refrain

Oh Non, Non, Non, Non, Oh, Oh Oh Oh Oh Oh
Le Noir & le Blanc ne s'unissent-ils pas
S'il te plait aime-moi, si tu veux que je t'aime moi

Hier ce Noir, c'était moi le type un certain genre de
    voyou
Y avait une fosse, un mur, un univers entre moi & vous
Hier je voulais tout cramer, le bourgeois je détestais
Ce Fabien j'ai depouillé j'ai kiffé de voir le bab flipper
Donne-moi ce que t'as sur toi ou bien je te plante "brêle"
Pour toi ça change quoi t'es qu'in sale petit-bourgeois
Hier sa vie je ne l'ai pas comprise mais après cette scène
J'ai gardé ma haine pourqoi nous on est pauvre et puis
    pas vous
Hier c'était ça nous comme beaucoup le savent
On était jaloux on haïssait le Blanc on était paumé
Esclave en Amerique on chanta la soul
Et puis y a eu colonialisme maintenant on est dans la
    zone
Vous allez payer pour ce qu'a subi l'Afrique
Ce hier, c'est le hier de tant de gens que la haine brise
Ce hier, c'est le hier de tant de Malik que la haine brise

Refrain

Aujourd'hui la couleur de ma peau n'est plus un
    drapeau
Juste un arc-en-ciel où se reflete l'universal
Aujourd'hui grace à l'Amour et le spirituel
Le Noir, le Blanc d'hier sont devenus des frères
On est tous or couleur miel quand on va vers la haut
La poésie de la vie a su me faire écrire ces mots

Aujourd'hui Fabien & Malik se donnent la main
Si la bêtise divise, la sagesse rend un
Aujourd'hui je sais que les fleurs n'ont pas toutes les
    même teinte
Du choix de la nature nous ne pouvons porter atteinte
Dieu a fait les differences non pas qu'on s'affronte
Les cultures sont des richesses pour que l'on se rencontre
En somme, ensemble on plane sur un tapis Volant
Le monde est devenu dune et sent le musc blanc
Fabien et moi avons pris ce même tapis Volant
Où le sang n'a qu'une couleur rouge couleur de l'Amour

Refrain

Ending
Oh Non, Non, Non, Non, Oh, Oh Oh Oh Oh Oh
Le Noir allume les lumières la nuit
Le Blanc éteint le sombre de nos tristes nuits
Que te dire sinon faut qu'on soit Ami
Noir & Blanc c'est la même je te l'ai déjà dit

Translation:

BLACK & WHITE

Ladies and gentlemen, music!

Intro
Oh No, No, No, No, Oh, Oh Oh Oh Oh Oh
The Black illuminates the lights at night
The White extinguishes the darkness of our sad nights
What can I say except we should be friends
Black & White it's the same thing as I've already told
    you

Let me tell you yesterday I was this White, such
    different red blood
I have lived so far from the other since I experienced
    this scene
A knife dirty petit-bourgeois give me all you got
Fear, rage cloistered me in hatred
Sown like this seed, brings about misfortune
So much vicissitude counted off by resentment
And hatred multiplies from it I am a prisoner
On one side and the other we all see this only brings
    about pain
All this is a common phenomenon
What I mean is it's just an epiphenomenon
The addition of this kind of event always leads toward
The subtraction of yesterday's noble sentiments
Dirty "bleep" fat "bleep" why don't you go "bleep"
    yourself
Go back to where you came from if you don't like it
    here
This yesterday is the yesterday of so many folk, with
    such different red blood

Refrain
Oh No, No, No, No, Oh, Oh Oh Oh Oh Oh
The Black and the White are not uniting
Please love me, if you want me to love you

Yesterday this Black, it was me typical example of a
    certain kind of thug
There was a moat, a wall, a universe between you and
    me
Yesterday I wanted to burn it all down, the bourgeois I
    detested

I picked this Fabien clean I got turned on seeing the
     Whitey flip out
Give me all you got on you or else I'll stab you dead
     "loser"
That will be a change for you huh, you are only a dirty
     petit-bourgeois
Yesterday I did not understand his life but after this
     scene
I kept my hatred because we are poor and you are not
Yesterday it was like this like lots of people know
We were jealous we hated Whitey we were lost
Slave in America we sang our soul
And then there was colonization today we are in the
     ghetto
You are going to pay for what Africa suffered
This yesterday, it is the yesterday of so many folk
     broken by hatred
This yesterday, it is the yesterday of so much Malik
     broken by hatred

Refrain

Today the color of my skin is no longer a flag
Just a rainbow reflecting the universal
Today thanks to Love and the spiritual
The Black, the White of yesterday have become
     brothers
Everyone is a golden honey yellow when rising toward
     the heights
Life's poetry taught me how to write these words
Today Fabien and Malik clasp hands
If stupidity divides wisdom makes one
Today I know that flowers are not all the same hue

We cannot strike a blow against the choices made by
    nature
God has created differences not to cause confrontation
Cultures offer riches so that we may meet one another
In sum, together we soar off on a flying carpet
The world's turned into dune and smells of white
    musk
Fabien and I took this same flying carpet
Where blood has only the color red the color of Love

Refrain

Ending
Oh No, No, No, No, Oh, Oh Oh Oh Oh Oh
The Black illuminates the lights at night
The White extinguishes the darkness of our sad nights
What can I say except we should be friends
Black and White it's the same thing as I've already told
    you

LA LANGAGE DU COEUR

Tout ce dont j'ai besoin c'est d'Amour voir le monde
    avec des yeux de velours
Mon ciel se dégage et le soleil bat dans ma poitrine
Tenir dans ma main le Coeur de ma femme et celui de
    mon fils
C'est agrandir ou bien réduire l'horizon d'êtres qui
    nous sont chers
Ma mère a dû ressentir cela lorsqu'elle nous voyait
    grandir et papa n'était pa là
Une chance qu'on ait pu voir que le monde était beau
Trop nombreux sont ceux qui croient vivre la tête sous
    l'eau
Et vont d'illusions en désillusions embourbés dans leurs
    passions
Va où ton Coeur te porte et tu trouveras le vrai
Vraiment j'ai vu des gens souffrir et partit mais
    malheureusement tous n'ont pas eu la chance de
    revenir
S'arreter sur la couleur ou les origines est une
    leurre
Un prison où s'enferment eux-mêmes ceux qui ont peur
    d'eux-mêmes
Dépasser la nostalgie du passé, la crainte du future
Profiter de chaque moment devient une aventure

Refrain
Voir la vie comme à mes cinq ans
Comblé dans les bras de maman
Cet Amour que je cherche
Guide chacun de mes gestes
Vouloir le grand Amour à seize ans

Lui donner la main à vingt ans
C'est d'Amour que je rêve

Regarde dans le coeur de celui qui aime la peur s'en va
En la religion de l'Amour j'ai mis ma foi
Aujourd'hui que tu sois juif, chrétien, ou bien
bouddhiste je t'aime
L'Amour est universal mais peu d'hommes saissent le
langage des oiseaux
Sinon la Paix illuminerait le monde comme un flambeau
Au lieu de ça des vies se brisent comme de verre fragile
Tout se mélange confusion entre l'important et le futile
Tout a un sens pour comprendre il s'agit d'ouvrir son coeur
Ne pas céder à l'horreur, se lever après l'erreur
Quand j'ai peur de ne pas être à la hauteur j'entends
Une voix me dire je suis l'Aimé et puis l'Amant
L'Amour comme seul vêtement comme le manteau du
Prophète
Si ta parole n'es pas plus belle que la silence faut que tu
te taises
Si tu arêtes juste un instant tu sauras si t'as tort
Qu'est-ce qui mérite sur cetter terre tes efforts

Refrain

Tout ce don't j'ai besoin c'est d'Amour pour pouvoir
vivre comme un homme libre
Enlever les entraves de la vie matérielle
Se débarrasser du superflu et aller ves l'essentiel
Bâtir des relations solides d'être à être
Déchirer chaque jour un peu plu la voile du paraître
Tout ce don't j'ai besoin c'est d'Amour pour me
connaître et puis les autres

Pour comprendre qu'on ne fait tous qu'un malgré le
  nombre
Et voir que le multiple finalement nous fait de l'ombre
Se séparer c'est dissocier la vague de l'océan
Quell vanité on est pur néant
Tout ce don't j'ai besoin c'est d'Amour, de Paix et
  d'Unité
Pour qu'on puisse communier dans l'Amour et le respect

Translation:

THE LANGUAGE OF THE HEART

All I need is Love to make sheep's eyes at the world
My sky clears up and the sun beats within my chest
Holding the Heart of my wife and that of my son in
  my hand
Is to expand or else shrink the horizons of individuals
  dear to us
My mother must have felt the same thing when she
  saw us growing up and papa was not there
Lucky we were to see that the world was beautiful
There are too many who live with their heads beneath
  the water
Going from illusion to disillusion bogged down in
  their passions
Go where your heart takes you and you shall discover
  what's true
For real I've seen people suffering and leaving but
  unfortunately not everyone has been lucky enough
  to come back
Getting stuck on colors or nationalities is a red herring
A prison in which those who are scared of themselves
  imprison themselves

To go beyond nostalgia for the past, the fear of the
   future
Take advantage of every moment becoming an
   adventure

Refrain
To see life like I did when I was five
Snuggled in my mother's arms
This Love I'm looking for
Guides every move I make
Wanting the great Love when I was sixteen
Giving my hand to it when I was twenty
It is Love of which I am dreaming

Look into the heart of someone who loves fear has left
I have placed my faith in the religion of Love
Today whether you are Jewish, Christian, or even
   Buddhist I love you
Love is universal but few men grasp the language of
   the birds
Otherwise Peace would light up the world like a torch
Instead of which lives are breaking like fragile glass
Everything is mixed-up confusion between the
   important and the futile
Everything has a meaning to be understood it is a
   question of opening its heart
Do not surrender to horror, get back on your feet after
   making a mistake
When I am scared of not being at my best I hear
A voice telling me I am loved and then the lover
Love my only vestment like the robe of the Prophet
If your words are no more beautiful than silence you
   need to shut up

If you stop for just a moment you will know that you
   were wrong
And what on this earth deserves your efforts

Refrain

All I need is Love to be able to live as a free man
To remove the shackles of material life
To get rid of the superfluous and go toward the
   essential
Build solid one-to-one relationships
Each day tear away a bit more of the veil of appearance
All I need is Love to know myself and then know
   others
To grasp that we are all only one despite how many we
   are in number
And see that the many in the end turns us into shadow
Separating is splitting the wave from the ocean
What vanity we are pure nothingness
All I need is Love, Peace, and Unity
So that we may share in Love and respect

ODE À L'AMOUR

Intro

Il y eut un temps où je faisais reproche à mon prochain
Si sa religion n'était pas proche a la mienne
Mais à present mon Coeur accueil tout forme
Il est une prairie pour les gazelles
Un cloître pour les moines
Un temple pour les idoles
Une Kaaba pour le pélerin
Les tables de la Torah at le livre du Coran
Je professe la religion de l'amour et quelle que soit
La direction que prenne sa monture, cette religion est
    ma religion et ma foi

J'ai pu voir qu'le livre de ma vie n'était pas seulement
    compose d'encre et des letters
Mon coeur devient blanc comme neige
Lorsque je goûte les saveurs du je t'aime
Dans ton jardin les fleurs sont multiple mais l'eau est
    unique
Laisse-moi vêtir de ton amour comme d'une tunique
Laisse-moi égrener le chapelet de mon Coeur dans ton
    souvenir
Laisse-moi crier au monde le parfum de mon désir
Le ciment de la providence nous lie comme les briques
    du secret
J'étais cuivre tu m'as rendu or toi l'Alchimiste de mon
    coeur
Toi qui as su gommer mes erreurs
Tu m'as tendu la main un jour et depuis je suis riche
Et il est pauvre celui qui vit dans ta niche
En vérité qui est le pauvre, qui est le riche?

Je partirais paré des joyaux tu m'a remis
N'est-ce pas toi Sidi qui m'a rendu vivant dans cette vie
(bis)

Refrain (bis)
L'amour un ocean sans fond, sans rivage
C'est le secret cache dans le Coeur du sage
De toute éternité tu as lié
La merveilleuse histoire de l'humanité

Mon Coeur fut transpercé par un rayon de soleil
Non pas l'étoile qui luit pour tous celle que les âmes
éveillent
N'est croyant que celui qui aime l'autre comme lui-
même
L'existence est un don mais trop peu de gens
s'émeri-veillent
Parce que les tenues qu'elle revêt ne sont jamais les
mêmes
Parce que l'apparence ne trompe que ceux qui s'y
arrêtent
J'ai bu le vin de l'Amour les gens sonts changés en
frères
Et me prennent pour fou ceux qui au lieu du coeur ont
une pierre
Verse-moi donc une autre coupe que je goûte enfin l'ivresse
Ce n'est qu'une métaphore pour ceux qui comprennent
J'ai compris ce qu'était le bien à la lueur de mon coeur
Et la sincérité seule nous préserve de l'erreur
Les actes ne valent que par les intentions à chacun selon
son but
Aimer l'autre quoi qu'il en coûte et envers soi mener la
lutte

Dans ma poitrine est enfoui le trésor des justes
Si y en a pour un partageons y en a pour tous

Et en vérité qui es-tu toi l'Amour, toi que je cherche
*   tant*
J'ai perçu tant de mirages qui de loin portaient ton nom
Réponds, tu es le trésor cache, cherché par l'Amant et
*   l'Aimé*
Mais ne le savent que ceux qui de toi sont épris
Je veux être de ceux dont le visage porte la marque de
*   ta proximité*
Leurs coeurs gémissent et tu les remplis du secret, du
*   miel de cette vie*
Tu brûles et tu soignes à la fois les maux
Et les mots me manquent pour oser dire
Que tu es la source de toutes choses
De toute éternité ces mots sont graves dans mon coeur
Je t'aime, je t'aime, je t'aime ô Amour
Sois-en sûr comme le soleil et la lune dechirent le ciel
Au cours de chacun de leurs passages
L'Amour est la courrone des actes
Fais de moi un roi pour que je puisse donner la pacte
Fais de moi un roi pour que je puisse donner la pacte

Translation:

ODE TO LOVE

Intro
Time was I would criticize my neighbor
If his religion was not the same as mine
But now my heart welcomes every form
It is a prairie for the gazelles and
A cloister for monks

A temple for idols and
A Kaaba for the pilgrim
The Tables of the Torah and the Book of the Qur'an
I follow the religion of Love and whatever
Direction taken by Love's camel, that is my religion
    and my faith.

I was able to see that the book of my life was not
    composed merely of ink and letters
My heart becomes white as snow
When I taste the savors of "I love you"
In your garden there are many flowers but only one
    water
Let me clad myself in your love like a tunic
Let me count off the rosary of my heart in your
    memory
Let me shout to the world the perfume of my desire
The cement of providence binds us like the bricks of
    the secret
I was copper you made me gold, alchemist of my heart
You who knew how to erase my mistakes
You extended your hand to me one day and since then
    I have been rich
And he is poor that one who lives in your niche
In truth who is the poor man and who is the rich?
I would depart adorned with the jewels you have given
    back to me
Isn't it you Sidi who brought me back to life in this
    life? *(repeat)*

Refrain (repeat)
Love is an ocean without bottom or shores
It is the secret hidden in the heart of the sage

Throughout eternity you have bound together
The marvelous history of humanity

My heart was pierced by a ray of sunlight
Not by the star that shines for all those whose souls
    have awakened
The only believer is the one who loves the other as
    himself
Existence is a gift but too few people find this amazing
Because the outfits it wears are never the same
Because appearances only deceive those who stop at
    them
I have drunk the wine of Love and people were
    changed into brothers
And I was taken for a madman by those who have a
    stone in the place of their heart
So fill me another cup that I may finally taste
    drunkenness
This is only a metaphor for those who understand
I understood that it was clearly the gleam of my own
    heart
And sincerity alone that spares us from error
Actions are only worth what each person intends by
    them in accordance with his purpose
To love the other whatever the cost and lead the battle
    against yourself
In my chest the treasure of the just is buried
If there is enough for one let's share it there is enough
    for all

In truth who are you Love, you I have sought so much?
I have seen so many mirages that from afar carried
    your name

Answer, you are the hidden treasure, sought by the
    lover and the beloved
But this is known only to those madly in love with you
I wish to be one of those whose face bears the mark of
    your proximity
Their hearts groan and you fill them with the secret,
    the honey of this life
You simultaneously burn and ease all ills
And words fail me to dare say
That you are the source of all things
For all eternity these words are etched upon my heart
I love you, I love you, I love you, O Love
Of this you may be as sure as the sun and moon
    rending the sky
During the course of each of their passages
Love is the crown of actions
Make me a king so that I can make the treaty
Make me a king so that I can make this treaty

DISCOGRAPHY AND DISTINCTIONS

‖‖‖‖‖‖‖‖‖‖‖‖‖‖‖‖‖‖‖‖‖‖‖‖‖‖‖‖‖

DISCOGRAPHY

With the Group NAP

Trop beau pour être vrai (maxi CD), High Skillz, 1994

La racaille sort un disque, High Skillz/Night & Day, 1996

Je viens des quartiers, High Skillz/Night & Day, 1997

La boulevard des rêves brisés, High Skillz/RCA/BMG, 1999

A l'intérieur de nous, Arista/BMG, 2000

Solo

Le face à face des coeurs, Atmosphériques/Universal, 2004

Gibraltar, Atmosphériques/Gibraltar/Universal, 2006; Prix
Constantin, 2006; Grand Prix Académie Charles Cros, 2006;
La Victoire de la Musique, 2007

Dante, Universal, 2008

Other

Last Night, with Moby, 2008

DISTINCTIONS

Abd al Malik is the recipient of the prestigious Chevalier des Arts et
des Lettres award, 2008, as well as the recipient of the Victoires de la
Musique award, 2008, for the best male artist of the year.

BOOKS OF RELATED INTEREST

Journey to the Lord of Power
A Sufi Manual on Retreat
by Ibn Arabi, with commentary by Abd al-Kerim al-Jili
Translated from the Arabic by Rabia Terry Harris

The Book of Sufi Healing
by Shaykh Hakim Moinuddin Chishti

The Spiritual Journey of Alejandro Jodorowsky
The Creator of *El Topo*
by Alejandro Jodorowsky

Muhammad
His Life Based on the Earliest Sources
by Martin Lings

Tales of a Modern Sufi
The Invisible Fence of Reality and Other Stories
by Nevit O. Ergin

The Forbidden Rumi
The Suppressed Poems of Rumi on Love, Heresy, and Intoxication
Translations and Commentary by Nevit O. Ergin and Will Johnson

The Rubais of Rumi
Insane with Love
Translations and Commentary by Nevit O. Ergin and Will Johnson

The Spiritual Practices of Rumi
Radical Techniques for Beholding the Divine
by Will Johnson

INNER TRADITIONS • BEAR & COMPANY
P.O. Box 388
Rochester, VT 05767
1-800-246-8648
www.InnerTraditions.com

Or contact your local bookseller